What's in the Bible and How Do I Use It?

What's in the Bible and How Do I USE iT ?

Real Help for Regular People

Abingdon Press
Nashville

WHAT'S IN THE BIBLE AND HOW DO I USE IT?

This book is printed on acid-free paper.

ISBN 978-0-687-65403-1

08 09 10 11 12 13 14 15 16 17—10 9 8 7 6 5 4 3 2 1
MANUFACTURED IN THE UNITED STATES OF AMERICA

Table of Contents

Welcome to
What's in the Bible and How Do I Use It?

Studying the Bible is an enriching, lifelong journey; but it can be a little intimidating if you are taking your first steps.

Inside these pages you will discover basic helps, like how to look up a verse and how the Bible is organized, as well as some simple framework, like important people, places, and events, that may help you put it all together. The material is presented in a straightforward, easy-to-understand manner, with fun facts and interesting trivia scattered throughout.

But more than lists of facts, this book is about delving into God's Word and finding that it is alive, powerful, and still speaks to us today. These tools may help you become comfortable and familiar with the Bible as an everyday companion and source of wisdom and joy.

You are off to a great start simply because you *have* started. Enjoy the journey!

Chapter 1:
How to Use the Bible

Choosing a Bible for Your Personal Study

Translations

Libraries and bookstores have shelves full of Bibles, and each version is a little different. There are King James Versions, Revised Standard Versions, Contemporary English Versions, and many others. These are called translations or paraphrases. Although each translation is the inspired Word of God, they use grammar and words in different ways so that everyone, at every level of life and experience, can understand the message of God.

Translations of the Hebrew text that we call the Old Testament began as early as fifth century B.C. The Aramaic language was at that time common in many Jewish communities, and the people needed the Hebrew law in a familiar language. By the third century B.C, the large Jewish community located in Egypt needed the Pentateuch translated into Greek, which had become their main language. By the end of the second century B.C, the entire Old Testament was probably translated into Greek.[1] By the third century A.D., the Greek Bible had been translated into Latin; and in the sixteenth century, the Latin Vulgate, the "common" version, was declared the authentic Bible of the Church.

The first English translation of the entire Bible was completed by John Wycliffe between 1380 and 1382. It, and others following, brought about great conflict since the general thought was that the Bible should be taught by authorities, not read by commoners.

In 1604, King James commissioned a new English translation of the Bible. He directed that it be translated from the Hebrew and Greek, and the language was to follow as closely as possible the familiar usage of earlier English Bibles. The King James Version of the Bible, originally published in 1611, remained the primary Bible for Christians for 300 years.[2]

Translation or Paraphrase?

A *formal equivalent,* or *word-for-word, translation* is one that reproduces the language of the original source as closely as possible. The King James Version is a word-for-word translation.

A *meaning-based functional equivalent translation* is concerned with the meaning, not the specific wording, of the original source. The New International Version is a meaning-based functional equivalent.

A *paraphrase* presents biblical accounts combined with the author's theological views. *THE MESSAGE* is a paraphrase.

How did the Bible get divided into chapters and verses?
The Archbishop of Canterbury Stephen Langton probably did the division of the Bible into the present chapters in the thirteenth century. Robert Stephanus in his Greek New Testament first published the New Testament's present verses in 1551. The first English translation with verse divisions was Whittington's translation in 1557. The first English Bible with Old and New Testaments divided into verses was the Geneva version of 1560.

A Few Well-known Translations
Contemporary English Version (CEV)—this contemporary-style Bible uses common language that can be easily understood when read and

heard aloud, not just when it is read silently. It is a good Bible for children, youth, and new Bible readers.

Good News Translation (GNT)— also known as Today's English Version or Good News Bible, uses a simplified, common form of the English language. It is commonly used for youth study groups and less formal worship services.

King James Version (KJV)—originally published in 1611 at the request of King James I of England, this Bible is perhaps the single most important book in shaping the modern English language. It is the most widely owned and used English translation in the USA.

New American Standard Bible (NASB)—said to be the most "word-for-word" translation available today, this is a good translation to use in formal Bible study.

New International Version (NIV)—one of the most popular Bibles in use today, this Bible is often used for individual study.

New Living Translation (NLT)—this revision of the Living Bible paraphrase is a reader-friendly translation for anyone, especially adults who study English as a second language.

New Revised Standard Version (NRSV)—this revision of the Revised Standard Version, published in 1989, is a standard translation for serious Bible study in seminaries and colleges.

Today's New International Version (TNIV)—has both updated language and more gender-sensitive language.

THE MESSAGE—this contemporary (the New Testament was completed in 1998 and the complete Bible in 2002) paraphrase is used by many individuals for inspirational study.

Look at the following verses in different translations:

John 3:16

NRSV

"For God so loved the world that he gave his only Son, so that everyone who believes in him may not perish but may have eternal life."

TNIV

"For God so loved the world that he gave his one and only Son, that whoever believes in him shall not perish but have eternal life."

THE MESSAGE

"This is how much God loved the world: He gave his Son, his one and only Son. And this is why: so that no one need be destroyed; by believing in him, anyone can have a whole and lasting life."

Psalm 23

NRSV

The LORD is my shepherd, I shall not want.
  He makes me lie down in green pastures;
he leads me beside still waters; he restores my soul.
He leads me in right paths for his name's sake.
Even though I walk through the darkest valley,
  I fear no evil;
for you are with me;
   your rod and your staff—
   they comfort me.
You prepare a table before me
  in the presence of my enemies;

you anoint my head with oil;
>my cup overflows.
Surely goodness and mercy shall follow me
>all the days of my life,
and I shall dwell in the house of the LORD
>my whole life long.

TNIV

The LORD is my shepherd, I lack nothing.
>He makes me lie down in green pastures,
he leads me beside quiet waters, he refreshes my soul.
He guides me along the right paths for his name's sake.
Even though I walk through the darkest valley,
>I will fear no evil,
for you are with me;
>your rod and your staff,
>they comfort me.
You prepare a table before me
>in the presence of my enemies.
You anoint my head with oil;
>my cup overflows.
Surely your goodness and love will follow me
>all the days of my life,
and I will dwell in the house of the LORD
>forever.

THE MESSAGE

God, my shepherd! I don't need a thing.
>You have bedded me down in lush meadows,
>you find me quiet pools to drink from.
>True to your word,
>you let me catch my breath
>and send me in the right direction.

Even when the way goes through
   Death Valley,
   I'm not afraid
      when you walk at my side.
   Your trusty shepherd's crook
      makes me feel secure.

You serve me a six-course dinner
      right in front of my enemies.
   You revive my drooping head;
      my cup brims with blessing.

Your beauty and love chase after me
      every day of my life.
   I'm back home in the house of God
      for the rest of my life.

- What differences in meaning do you find in the different versions?
- Which versions do you prefer? Why?

Topping the Top Ten

Not only is the Bible the best-selling book of all time, it also is the best-selling book of the year, every year.[3] A conservative estimate shows that:

- Americans purchased some 25 million Bibles in 2005
- More than half a billion dollars is spent on Bibles each year[4]

New twentieth-century translations seek to bring the biblical text to people today in ways that are accurate and also easier for modern-day people to read. In 1966, The American Bible Society published *Good News for Modern Man*, a New Testament geared toward the young, non-churchgoer. After only a year, the Bible that looked like a paperback novel had sold more than 5 million copies.

Another very popular translation, the New International Version, published by Zondervan in 1973. The scholars leading the translation wanted an accurate translation that offered the clarity and literary quality that would work well in preaching, private reading, and worship. The New Testament was followed by a complete Bible in 1978.

The Revised Standard Version, first appearing in 1946, was followed by the New Revised Standard Version (NRSV) in 1989. The copyright holders, the National Council of Churches, wanted the NRSV to offer more accuracy and clarity, bringing all the available new learnings and scholarship to the task. They also had a goal of eliminating masculine-oriented language relating to people when it could be done without changing the context of the passages. (For example, Matthew 5:11 begins, "blessed are you when people revile you..." rather than the previous translation "blessed are you when men revile you...")

▶ *FAST FACT:* **Who reads the Bible more, men or women?** 49% of women have read the Bible in the past week, compared to 35% of men who report reading the Bible in the past week—according to the 2007 survey of The Barna Group.[5]

How to Choose a Bible

A variety of Bibles are on the market. They focus on theology, historical context, or practical applications of biblical teachings. They are for new believers, biblical scholars, couples, brides, surfers, and cowboys. So how can you possibly know what Bible to choose?

First, consider the Bible translation your church or study group is using. Then ask yourself these questions:

- Do I plan to use the Bible at church, during group studies, and/or at home?
- Do I want the Bible to have notes and study tools in it, or will I use a concordance and other reference books for study?
- Is it easy for me to read and understand the language of the Bible translation that I am considering?
- Which do I enjoy more—the idea of word-for-word accuracy from the Hebrew and Greek translation or the readability and beauty of the language?

Computer Software

When choosing a Bible, you might want to think about also choosing a Bible for your computer. There are several advantages when studying at home or in an area where you are comfortable using your computer. The computer software uses sound, graphics, and modern technology to bring biblical stories to life. Some software has the capability to give side-by-side comparisons of different verse translations.

▶ *FAST FACT:* Research shows that 91% of American households own at least one Bible (most households average four), meaning that Bible publishers sell 25 million copies a year of a book that almost everybody already has.[6]

▶ *FAST FACT:* According to a survey by the Thomas Nelson Publishing Company, more than 60% of Bibles are purchased as gifts.[7]

How to Find a Reference

The commonly accepted way to cite a Bible reference includes the name of the book, the chapter number, and the verse number. For example, Luke 24:1 refers to the Easter story in the Gospel of Luke, twenty-fourth chapter, first verse.

Now, look in the front of your Bible. There you will find a table of contents that lists the books of the Bible and the page numbers where they begin. Many Bibles include an alphabetical list as well as a numerical list.

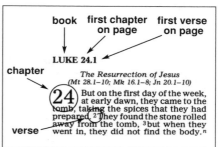

Thumbing Through the Bible

As you become familiar with the Bible, it will be helpful to remember:

- The Old Testament is about the first two-thirds of the Bible.
- Psalms is about in the middle of the Bible.
- The Gospels are the first four books of the New Testament.
- Revelation is the last book of the Bible.

Three Helpful Resources

Bible Concordance. This book, arranged in alphabetical order, can help you find a specific Bible reference. Some concordances provide brief information about the meaning and context of a listed word.

Bible Dictionary. Much the same as a general dictionary, a Bible dictionary focuses on biblical terms. Many words are defined and Scripture references are given.

Bible Commentary. Commentaries are often multiple volumes and resemble an encyclopedia of biblical interpretation presented by one or more writers.

How the Bible Is Organized

The Old Testament

The first 39 books of the Bible are called the Old Testament. It is the record of the beginning of the world and of humankind. Here we learn about God's interaction with Abraham and the creation of the nation of Israel. The oldest collection of this material into a written record (which included oral traditions, songs, sayings and narrative) dates from the time of David and Solomon around 1000 B.C. The Old Testament has four major divisions: the law, the history, wisdom, and the prophets.[8]

The First Five Books

- The first five books of the Bible are called Torah and Pentateuch, which was established between the sixth and fourth centuries B.C.[9]
- *Torah* is the Hebrew word for "law" or "teaching instruction."
- *Pentateuch* comes from two Greek words: *penta*, meaning "five," and *teuchos*, meaning "vessel" or "container." The Bible was first written on rolls of papyrus and kept in cylinders. By A.D. 100, scribes used codices, pages of papyrus bound at one end, which provided for easier transportation and cross-referencing.

Books of Moses and the Law

Genesis
Exodus
Leviticus
Numbers
Deuteronomy

History books

Joshua
Judges
Ruth
1 Samuel
2 Samuel
1 Kings

2 Kings
1 Chronicles
2 Chronicles
Ezra
Nehemiah
Esther

Wisdom books

Job
Psalms
Proverbs
Ecclesiastes
Song of Solomon

Prophets' books

Isaiah
Jeremiah
Lamentations
Ezekiel
Daniel
Hosea
Joel
Amos
Obadiah

Jonah
Micah
Nahum
Habakkuk
Zephaniah
Haggai
Zechariah
Malachi

The New Testament

All 27 books of the New Testament are about Jesus Christ, the Son of God. The New Testament is a record of Jesus' life on earth and an instruction manual for how we can have a personal relationship with God through Jesus. Written in the first century A.D., the New Testament is divided into five parts: the Gospels; history of the early church; Paul's letters; other letters; and the Apocalypse (Revelation).

Gospels
Matthew
Mark
Luke
John

History of the Early Church
Acts of the Apostles

Paul's Letters

Romans	1 Thessalonians
1 Corinthians	2 Thessalonians
2 Corinthians	1 Timothy
Galatians	2 Timothy
Ephesians	Titus
Philippians	Philemon
Colossians	Hebrews

Other Letters
James
1 Peter
2 Peter
1 John
2 John
3 John
Jude

Apocalypse
Revelation

Not until the second century A.D. did Christians set apart specifically Christian writings and treat them as equal to the Hebrew Scriptures by reading them in worship. A New Testament canon, or list of religious writings, developed gradually. The earliest listing of books identical to our present New Testament canon was prepared by Athanasius of Alexandria in A.D. 367.[10]

How to Study the Bible

"Do your best to present yourself to God as one approved by him, a worker who has no need to be ashamed, rightly explaining the word of truth." (2 Timothy 2:15)

When studying the Bible, be careful to seek the truth of Scripture and guard against interpreting verses to support your own personal beliefs. Seek the true meaning of the words that were inspired by God.

Principles for Bible Study With Others
Reading and studying the Bible on your own is a great experience; but hopefully, you may also have the opportunity to be part of a group study. In group study, you'll hear the viewpoints of others. You may not always agree with everyone in your group, but studying together offers new insights and viewpoints to carry you farther on your journey.

Here are a few guidelines to think about when studying the Bible with other people:

1. The Word of God is Jesus Christ, and the words of the Bible tell us about that Word. Therefore, when we study the words of the Bible we always look behind, in, and through those words for God's Word—Jesus Christ.

2. No Christian has a monopoly on understanding either God's Word or the words of the Scripture. This includes biblical scholars and the Christian just beginning study. All of us must listen to one another as we seek to understand the richness of God's gifts.

3. We assume that we will each arrive at different understandings of portions of Scripture and that that will not disturb God as much as it will some of us.

4. Few of us know Hebrew or Greek, and we therefore need to use a variety of English versions to try to understand the text.

5. Different biblical understandings can remain among us, but we can still be Christian friends. In fact, as we grow to better understand our differences, we can grown in our appreciation of one another.[11]

Five Tips for Studying the Bible

1. Ask God to guide your study and open your heart to God's Word.

2. Use a notebook and pen or pencil to take notes and write down questions that you might want to discuss with another Christian.

3. Have a regular, private place for your Bible studies.

4. Read a study passage in context, studying the verses and chapters before and after it.

5. Use a Bible dictionary and/or concordance to help you with words and their meaning(s) and the general time frame in history.

As you study the Bible, write the answers to these questions in your notebook:

- what does the passage you are studying clearly say?
- what does the passage you are studying *not* say?
- who was the target audience that the author was writing to?
- who wrote the book in which you find this passage?

- is the passage written as a parable or allegory? Does it contain symbolism, poetry, metaphors, and other figures of speech? (See also the discussion on Literary Devices in Chapter 2, pages 31–34.)

Some persons become quickly discouraged when they attempt to read the Bible. They find many portions of the Bible difficult to understand. Not all sections are vitally important for the modern reader to grasp. For example, much of the legal code contained in Leviticus is irrelevant to today's situations. However, other passages urgently need to be read and yet are difficult to understand.

Some bits of advice when reading the Bible becomes difficult:

- Don't give up.
- Try to gain a sense of the major themes of the Bible before attempting to work through the Bible verse by verse.
- Trying using Bible study tools (see suggestions, pages 17–18).
- Use your imagination to envision yourself among the participants in the Bible story or among the first readers of the Bible passage.[12]

Reading the Bible in a Year

The Bible is a big book, and some may find the thought of reading the Bible cover to cover overwhelming. Fortunately, there are now many plans available to help you read the Bible through in a year. These plans break the Bible into shorter segments for brief daily readings.

For an easy-to-follow plan to read the entire Bible through in a year, see the suggested schedule on pages 105–09.

▶ **FAST FACT:** The evangelical polling firm, The Barna Group, says 47% of Americans read the Bible every week.[13]

It's All in the Numbers

- The Book of Numbers says 601,730 Israelites were counted in a census.
- Naaman dipped himself in the Jordan 7 times (2 Kings 5:10).
- The priests and soldiers marched around Jericho 7 times (Joshua 6:4).
- The psalmist praised God 7 times (Psalm 119:164).
- There were 12 tribes of Israel (Genesis 49:28).

Just how big was Goliath? Goliath stood "six cubits and a span" which translates to a little over nine feet tall.

- There were 12 disciples (Matthew 10:1).
- The Flood lasted 40 days and 40 nights (Genesis 7:17).
- Jonah warned Nineveh for 40 days (Jonah 3:4).
- Jesus fasted in the wilderness for 40 days and 40 nights (Matthew 4:2).
- Judas betrayed Jesus for 30 pieces of silver (Matthew 26:15).
- "Do not be afraid" is repeated 365 times in the Bible.
- King Solomon had 1,400 chariots and 12,000 horses stationed in the chariot cities and with the king in Jerusalem (1 Kings 10:26).

The Firsts
- Stephen was the first Christian martyr (Acts 6:8 8:2).
- Cain was the first farmer (Genesis 4:2).
- Abel was the first murder victim (Genesis 4).

How Many Wives Did David Have?
8 plus several concubines
His wives included: Ahinoam, Abigail, Maacah, Haggith, Abital, Eglah, Bathsheba (also called Bath-shua), and Michal. (2 Samuel 3:2-5; 5:14-16; 1 Chronicles 3:5-8)

24

Weights and Measurements

Here is a list of biblical units of measurements and their approximate modern-day equivalents.

BIBLICAL UNIT	APPROX. AMERICAN EQUIVALENT	APPROX. METRIC EQUIVALENT
WEIGHTS		
talent (60 minas)	75 pounds	34 kilograms
mina (50 shekels)	1 ¼ pounds	0.6 kilogram
shekel (2 bekas)	2/5 ounce	11.5 grams
pim (2/3 shekel)	1/3 ounce	7.6 grams
beka (10 gerahs)	1/5 ounce	5.5 grams
gerah	1/50 ounce	0.6 gram
LENGTH		
cubit	18 inches	0.5 meter
span	9 inches	23 centimeters
handbreadth	3 inches	8 centimeters
CAPACITY		
Dry Measure		
cor [homer] (10 ephahs)	6 bushels	220 liters
lethek (5 ephahs)	3 bushels	110 liters
ephah (10 omers)	3/5 bushel	22 liters
seah (1/3 ephah)	7 quarts	7.3 liters
omer (1/10 ephah)	2 quarts	2 liters
cab (1/18 ephah)	1 quart	1 liter
Liquid Measure		
bath (1 ephah)	6 gallons	22 liters
hin (1/6 bath)	4 quarts	4 liters
log (1/72 bath)	1/3 quart	0.3 liter

Can You Name the Sons of David?

Amnon, Chileab, Absalom, Adonijah, Shephatiah, Ithream, Solomon, Shammua, Shimea, Shobab, Nathan, Ibhar, Elishama, Eliphelet, Nogah, Nepheg, Japhia, Eliada, Elishama, Eliphelet (2 Samuel 3:2-5; 5:14-16; 1 Chronicles 3:5-8)

Ages

- Adam was 130 when Cain was born.
- Noah was 600 years old at the beginning of the Flood.
- Methuselah lived to be 969 years old.

How many wives did Solomon have? King Solomon had 700 wives plus 300 concubines (1 Kings 11:3). And he was considered wise.

---

[1] *The New Interpreter's Study Bible* (Abingdon, 2003); pp. 2244–45.

[2] Daniel Radosh, "The Good Book Business," *The New Yorker*, Dec. 18, 2006; http://www.newyorker.com/archive/2006/12/18/061218fa_fact1.

[3] Radosh, "The Good Book Business."

[4] Radosh, "The Good Book Business."

[5] "The Bible," The Barna Group, Ltd.; http://www.barna.org//flexpage.aspx?page=topic&topicid=7.

[6] Radosh, "The Good Book Business."

[7] Radosh, "The Good Book Business."

[8] *Cambridge Annotated Study Bible*, New Revised Standard Version (Cambridge University Press, 1993); p. 30–31.

[9] Adapted from DISCIPLE: BECOMING DISCIPLES THROUGH BIBLE STUDY, Study Manual, Second Edition (Abingdon, 1993); pp. 8–9. Used by permission.

[10] Adapted from DISCIPLE: BECOMING DISCIPLES THROUGH BIBLE STUDY, Study Manual, Second Edition (Abingdon, 1993); p. 9. Used by permission.

[11] Adapted from *Strengthening the Adult Sunday School Class*, by Dick Murray. Copyright © 1981 Abingdon Press. Adapted by permission.

[12] Adapted from *Get Acquainted With Your Bible*. Copyright © 1993 Abingdon Press. Used by permission.

[13] Radosh, "The Good Book Business."

Chapter 2:
Bible History

The Origin

There are more than 14,000 existing Old Testament manuscripts and fragments. There are more than 5,300 known copies and fragments of New Testament manuscripts in the original Greek.[1]

The first New Testament manuscripts were written on papyrus leaves; however, the manuscripts quickly became brittle and deteriorated. Only fragments of the original papyrus manuscripts remain. Scribes began using parchment to transcribe the Bible during the fourth century. It took another 800 years before paper was used to record biblical writings.

The Old Testament has...
- 39 books
- 929 chapters
- 23,214 verses
- 593,493 words
- Longest book: Psalms
- Shortest book: Obadiah (3rd shortest book in the Bible)

The New Testament has...
- 27 books
- 260 chapters

- 7,959 verses
- 181,253 words
- Longest book: Acts
- Shortest book in the Bible: 3 John (fewest number of words / 2 John has more words, but fewer verses.)
- 5 history books (Acts and the Gospels: Matthew, Mark, Luke, John)
- 21 letters (epistles)
- 1 book of prophecy (Revelation)

The Old and the New

Many biblical scholars say that Job, written as early as 1000 B.C., is the oldest book in the Bible, and the Book of Revelation, written around A.D. 95, is the youngest.

The Dead Sea Scrolls

First discovered in the late 1940s, the Dead Sea Scrolls consist of approximately 1,000 documents, including texts from the Hebrew Bible. These scrolls were found in caves near the ruins of an ancient settlement on the northwest shore of the Dead Sea.

The most extraordinary of the scrolls is the Isaiah Scroll, found relatively intact and 1,000 years older than any previously known copy of Isaiah.

Today, the Dead Sea Scrolls are made available to the public through monitored exhibits. The Shrine of the Books in Israel was built in 1965 specifically to preserve and exhibit the scrolls. Because of the age and condition of the scrolls, they are displayed using a rotating system so that exposure to light is limited. Not all of the scrolls are housed at the Shrine; some are kept at the Rockefeller Museum in Jerusalem, while yet others are in Jordan and Europe.

Apocryphal Writings

The Old Testament Apocrypha contains writings from the period between the Old and New Testaments. These books are included in the Greek translation of the Old Testament, called the Septuagint, but are not included in the Hebrew Bible. The Roman Catholic Church has accepted these books as canonical Scripture—that is, these books are included in their official Bible; Protestant churches have not. The Apocryphal books are as follows:

Tobit
Judith
Esther (the Greek version contains additional chapters)
The Wisdom of Solomon
Sirach
Baruch
The Letter of Jeremiah
The Additions to Daniel
1 Maccabees
2 Maccabees
1 Esdras
The Prayer of Manasseh
Psalm 151
3 Maccabees
2 Esdras
4 Maccabees

Why Some Books Made It Into the Bible... And Some Did Not

Have you ever wondered how and when the Bible was finally "final"? Fourth-century church leaders decided which writings would be standard Christian Scriptures based on three important criteria: the soundness of their teaching; the association of the writing with one of the first apostles; their general usage throughout the church of that time.

Hanukah—The Jewish celebration of Hanukah, also known as the Festival of Lights, is alluded to in the Apocryphal books of 1 and 2 Maccabbees. Both books mention an eight-day celebration and this eight-day event is established in 1 Maccabees as an event to be celebrated every year.

Some decisions were controversial. For example, the Book of Revelation, which was associated with the apostle John, almost was not included in the Bible because of its strange, difficult imagery. The "canon"—the official list of books considered authoritative as Scripture—was finally closed around the end of the fourth century.[3]

The Authorship of the Bible

The Bible, inspired by God, is both human and divine. You may be surprised at how human the Bible is when you read of violence, rape, betrayal, adultery, sickness, and death. Nothing is hidden. You also will be overwhelmed at how divine the Bible is when you see repentance and faith, just and compassionate laws, acts of devotion and self-sacrifice, and the unending love of the forgiving, covenant God.

Not only are the experiences both human and divine, but so are the actual writings. Oral tradition was finally put into writing, then edited and reedited, copied and recopied; the whole process is a witness to the guiding hand of God. Even the canonizing—setting the standards for what is Scripture—was inspired.

When we speak of Scripture as being inspired, we are recognizing that the Scriptures were written by particular persons in particular circumstances. We are saying that the Scriptures are connected to God and because of that connection, the Scriptures have power to bring about an encounter between God and the one who reads Scripture. The authority of Scripture, then, lies in its ability to cause encounter. When we read the Bible and God speaks to us, we hear the Bible as God's Word.[4]

Scholars have spent much time researching and contemplating who wrote the various books of the Bible. Authorship is apparent for some books; scholars agree on the authorship of others; but the authorship of some books remains a mystery.

Literary Devices

The 66 books of the Bible contain a variety of literary devices. From dialogue to soliloquy, from prose to poetry. When studying the Bible, it is helpful to look at the literary devices used for the verses you are reading. Language usage can give you a clue as to what the author is trying to convey.

Hyperbole—exaggeration used purposefully to illustrate a point or idea
Matthew 23:24 ("You blind guides! You strain out a gnat but swallow a camel!") is perhaps the most memorable use of hyperbole in the New Testament.

In Luke 14:26 Jesus says, "Whoever comes to me and does not hate father and mother, wife and children, brothers and sisters, yes, and even life itself, cannot be my disciple." Then on the other hand, Matthew 19:19 says, "Honor your father and mother; also, you shall love your neighbor as yourself." So, what are we to do?

Luke 14:26 is an example of the numerous times that the literary form hyperbole is used in the Bible. Jesus is using exaggeration to emphasize his point. The point, in this verse, is that pleasing God must come before pleasing anyone else, no matter how close we are to the other person.

Look at these other examples of hyperbole. What is Jesus really saying in these verses? If you do not understand these verses or others like them, read the verses in another Bible translation, seek out explanations in a Bible commentary, or ask another Christian to help you understand: Matthew 5:29; 7:3-4; 19:23-36.

Irony—*a statement or action with apparent meaning contrary to what is said*
Job used irony when speaking in Job 12:2: "No doubt you are the people, and wisdom will die with you." His biting comment communicated the opposite of what he literally said.

Metaphor—*one example used to represent another*
In biblical texts, often references to eating and drinking are used as metaphors for learning spiritual truths. Water, representing truth and knowledge, is perhaps the most frequently used metaphor in the Old Testament.

Jesus used many metaphors when he taught his disciples and the crowds. Look up these verses:

John 3:19; 4:14; 7:37; Mark 4:14, 20; Luke 8:11, 16; Revelation 7:17; Romans 13:12; 2 Corinthians 9:10

What words or phrases are used as metaphors in these passages? What do these figures of speech stand for?

Parable—*short, fictitious narrative*
One of the most recognizable literary devices used in the Bible is the parable. Jesus used brief and often simple narratives to illustrate moral lessons. The Parable of the Good Seed, the Prodigal Son, and the Parable of the Mustard Seed are examples.

Poetry—*verse, whether rhymed or unrhymed*
When thinking about poetry in the Bible, Psalms or the Song of Solomon come to mind; however, poetry is found in many books of the Bible. Take a look at John 1:1-14 and 1 Samuel 2:1-10.

▶ *FAST FACT:* Five Old Testament books of poetry are: Job, Psalms, Proverbs, Ecclesiastes, and Song of Solomon.

Riddle—*hidden saying*
Israelites commonly used riddles in their everyday conversations, so it is not unusual to find riddles in the Bible. One of the oldest recorded riddles was issued by Samson in Judges 14:14—"He said to them, 'Out of the eater came something to eat. Out of the strong came something sweet.'" (Read the story and find out what trouble speaking in riddles can cause.)

Do you know anyone who speaks in riddles? Someone who answers a question with a question? Take a look at John 4:7-26. As you read this Scripture, think about how you would feel if a stranger spoke to you in such a way. Would you be suspicious or trusting? Frustrated or curious? What was the Samaritan woman's response?

Today, as we read the conversation between Jesus and the Samaritan woman, we might feel a little aggravated—*why didn't Jesus just come out and tell her who he was?* However, as we read and study biblical text, we need to remember that customs and the manner in which people communicate have changed. It was common for people to answer one question with another question in biblical times. Knowing this, we can understand that the Samaritan woman was interested in learning from Jesus.

Chronology

Determining the date when biblical books were written is an ongoing project for many scholars; however, one generally accepted estimate is:

Gospel of Mark: A.D. +70 (conservative dating may be as early as 50)
Gospel of Matthew: A.D. +80–90 (conservative dating in the 60s although as early as the 40s)
Gospel of Luke: A.D. +85–105 (conservative dating in the 60s)
Gospel of John: A.D. +95–110 (conservative dating in the late 80s to early 90s)
Acts: A.D. +85–105 (conservative dating in 60s)
James: ca. A.D. 70–200 (conservative dating ca. A.D. 45–62)
Colossians: A.D. +60
Corinthians: A.D. +57
Ephesians: A.D. +65

Hebrews: A.D. +60–90

Epistles of John: A.D. +95–110

Jude: A.D. +70–100 (conservative dating in the 60s or earlier)

First Peter: ca. A.D. 90–96 (conservative dating ca. A.D. 64)

Second Peter: A.D. 100–140 (conservative dating ca. A.D. 64)

Philemon: A.D. +56

Philippians: A.D. +57–62

Romans: A.D. +57–58

Galatians: A.D. +54–55 (conservative dating in the late 40s)

Thessalonians: A.D. +50

Timothy: A.D. +70–100 (conservative dating ca. 60)

Titus: A.D. +70–100 (conservative dating ca. 60)

Revelation: A.D. +81–96 (dating in the 60s as a minority view among conservatives)

▶ *FAST FACT:* The Book of Psalms is the most quoted Old Testament book in the New Testament. It is quoted more than 70 times. The runner up? The Book of Isaiah is quoted approximately 50 times.

▶ *FAST FACT:* The Book of Esther is the only Old Testament book that does not mention God.

▶ *FAST FACT:* The Book of Obadiah is the shortest book in the Old Testament with only one chapter and 21 verses.

The Long and Short of It

Psalms is the longest book in the Bible

2 John is the shortest book in the Bible

Psalm 119 is the longest chapter in the Bible

Psalm 117 is the shortest chapter in the Bible

Esther 8:9 is the longest verse in the Bible

John 11:35 is the shortest verse in the Bible

[1]"Origin of the Bible: Credible & Authentic"; http://www.allabouttruth.org/origin-of-the-bible.htm.

[2]"Facts on the Bible"; http://bibleresources.bible.com/afacts.php.

[3]Adapted from *Get Acquainted With Your Bible*. Copyright ©1993 Abingdon Press. Used by permission.

[4]Adapted from DISCIPLE: BECOMING DISCIPLES THROUGH BIBLE STUDY, Study Manual, Second Edition (Abingdon, 1993); p. 8. Used by permission.

Chapter 3:
Where to Find…

Your Bible is a study tool. Do not be afraid to underline favorite passages and use sticky notes to mark Psalms, the beginning of the New Testament, the Ten Commandments, Jesus' parables, the Lord's Prayer, or other subjects that are important to your study. Some people use colored pencils to mark passages; for example, green to underline verses about money, red to underline verses about love, and so forth.

Look up the following Scriptures to practice using your Bible:

Genesis 1:1-31 — The Creation Story
Exodus 20:3-17 — The Ten Commandments
Psalm 23 — "The Lord is my shepherd …"
Matthew 7:12; Luke 6:21 — The Golden Rule
John 3:16 — "For God so loved the world …"

Famous Stories

Adam and Eve — Genesis 1–4
Noah's Ark and the Great Flood — Genesis 11
Moses parts the Red Sea — Genesis 14
Joseph and his Coat — Genesis 37
The Plagues — Exodus 7–12
David and Goliath — 1 Samuel 17
Jesus' Birth — Luke 2
Feeding of the 5,000 — Matthew 14:15-21; Mark 6:30-44; Luke 9:10

Last Supper

Matthew 26:17-30;
Mark 14:12-26; Luke 22:7-20

Jesus' Crucifixion

Matthew 27; Mark 15;
Luke 23; John 18:28-40

The Ten Commandments

God's Exclusive Claims
1. No Other Gods (Exodus 20:2-3)
2. No Image of God (Exodus 20:4-6)
3. No Misuse of God's Power (Exodus 20:7)

God's Basic Institutions
4. No Work on the Seventh Day (Exodus 20:8-11)
5. No Contempt for the Family (Exodus 20:12)

Basic Human Obligations
6. No Contempt for Human Life (Exodus 20:13)
7. No Contempt for Sex (Exodus 20:14)

Basic Social Obligations
8. No Contempt for the Goods of the Community (Exodus 20:15)
9. No Contempt for the Community's Institutions (Exodus 20:16)
10. No Lusting After the Life or Goods of Others (Exodus 20:17)[1]

The Teachings and Stories of Jesus

You will find the stories of Jesus' life in the Gospels—the first four books of the New Testament—Matthew, Mark, Luke, and John. Read these stories in your Bible and answer the following questions:
1. Where was Jesus born? (Luke 2:4-7)
2. Who visited Jesus when he was born? (Luke 2:16-18)

3. What was Jesus' occupation? (Mark 6:3)
4. Who were Jesus' disciples? (Matthew 4)
5. Where was Jesus when he turned water into wine? (John 2:1-12)

Five Parables of Jesus

Jesus often told stories about everyday life to teach the people around him. Here are five of the many parables that he told. Look them up in your Bible.

The good Samaritan	Luke 10:30-37
The lost/prodigal son	Luke 15:11-32
The mustard seed	Matthew 13:31-32; Luke 13:18-19
The lost sheep	Matthew 18:11-14; Luke 15:3-7
The house built on the rock	Matthew 7:24-27; Luke 6:47-49

The Sermon on the Mount

When Jesus taught his disciples and the large crowd with them in the Sermon on the Mount (Matthew 5; 6; 7), he included many important lessons. Two of those lessons are the Beatitudes and the Lord's Prayer.

The Beatitudes (Matthew 5:3-11)

"Blessed are the poor in spirit, for theirs is the kingdom of heaven.
Blessed are those who mourn, for they will be comforted.
Blessed are the meek, for they will inherit the earth.
Blessed are those who hunger and thirst for righteousness, for they
     will be filled.
Blessed are the merciful, for they will receive mercy.
Blessed are the pure in heart, for they will see God.
Blessed are the peacemakers, for they will be called children of God.
Blessed are those who are persecuted for righteousness' sake, for
     theirs is the kingdom of heaven.
Blessed are you when people revile you and persecute you and utter
     all kinds of evil against you falsely on my account."

The Lord's Prayer (Matthew 6:9-15)

"Our Father in heaven, hallowed be your name. Your kingdom come. Your will be done, on earth as it is in heaven. Give us this day our daily bread. And forgive us our debts, as we also have forgiven our debtors. And do not bring us to the time of trial, but rescue us from the evil one. For if you forgive others their trespasses, your heavenly Father will also forgive you; but if you do not forgive others, neither will your Father forgive your trespasses."

---

[1]Based on the grouping and summary of the Commandments found throughout *The Ten Commandments and Human Rights*, by Walter Harrelson (Fortress Press, 1980).

Chapter 4:
People

The Bible has a full cast of characters. There are kings, queens, judges, warriors, farmers, seamstresses, prophets, preachers, tax collectors, thieves, murderers, rich people, and poor people. Every type of person you can think of can be found in the Bible. Included in this chapter are just a few of the people you need to know.

Six Names for God
God has several names in the Bible. Here are six that you will see:
- Adonai, Lord and Master (Psalm 2:4)
- Creator (Genesis 1:1)
- El Shaddai, All Powerful (Genesis 17:1-2)
- Yahweh (Exodus 3:13-15)
- LORD (1 Samuel 1:3)
- Abba, Father (Mark 14:36)

What's in a Name?
The several different names used to refer to the people of God in the Bible can be confusing. For example, throughout the Book of Exodus, the words *Hebrew* and *Israelite* seem to be used interchangeably. Here is an attempt at making some distinctions:

Hebrews: an ethnic group that migrated from Mesopotamia into Canaan about 2100 B.C. At some point, they also become known as Israelites; and the two terms are synonymous for Christian Bible Study. Technically, the Hebrews were the descendants of Eber, great grandson of Shem, son of Noah, according to Genesis 10–11.

Israelites: members of the twelve Hebrew tribes that settled in Canaan following the Exodus from Egypt and the wandering through the wilderness of the Sinai Peninsula. These twelve tribes were said to be descended from the twelve sons of Jacob, who was also known as Israel. Hence, the "children" or descendants of Israel/Jacob were known as Israelites. When the kingdom of Israel divided into two portions in 922 B.C., the Northern Kingdom became known as Israel.

Judeans: the inhabitants of the Southern Kingdom of Judah, following the division of the United Kingdom of Israel. After the Babylonian Exile of 586-538 B.C. and the conquest of the area by Persians and Greeks, this southern region became known as Judea.

Jews: the people of Israel after the Exile. In the New Testament persons might be called Jews by reason of either nationality or religion. Today, the term *Jews* still refers to members either of the ethnic group or the religion.

NOTE: The term *Israeli* should only be used to refer to a citizen or inhabitant of the modern nation-state of Israel, which was founded in A.D. 1948.[1]

Ten Famous People of the Old Testament and Where to Find Them...

Adam and Eve	Genesis 1
Abraham	Genesis 11:26; Galatians 3:6-7; James 2:23
Isaac	Genesis 21:1-7; 25:19-28

Jacob	Genesis 27:1-40; 28:1–29
Moses	Exodus 2-4
David	1 Samuel; 2 Samuel
Job	Book of Job
Jeremiah	Book of Jeremiah

Joseph's Body Embalmed; Children of Israel Move Him 430 Years Later

When another key person of the Old Testament, Joseph, became old and ill, he gathered his brothers to him and made them promise that whenever God returned them to the Promised Land, that his body would go with them (Genesis 50:22-26). So, they embalmed his body, and placed it in a coffin. Then 430 years later, Moses made sure they took Joseph's body with them when the Exodus began (Exodus 13:19). Joseph was buried in the Promised Land (Joshua 24:32).

A Dozen Famous People of the New Testament and Where to Find Them...

Jesus Christ is without question the most famous person in the New Testament. Stories of the life and teachings of Jesus make up the first four books that we call the Gospels. Here are some other key figures:

Mary and Joseph	Luke 2:1
John the Baptist	Matthew 3; Mark 6:17-29
Martha and Mary	Luke 10:38-42
Mary Magdalene	John 20:1-18
Paul and Timothy	Acts 16:1-3; 19:22; 1 Timothy; 2 Timothy
Priscilla and Aquila	Acts 18:1-21, 24-28
Lazarus	John 11:1-45

Jesus' Disciples

The story of Jesus calling his 12 disciples is found in Matthew 4:18-22; 9:9; and John 1:35-51.

Zerubbabel [ze-RUB-uh-bul] led the first band of Jews out of their Babylonian captivity. When they returned to Jerusalem, they found the Temple and the wall that surrounded it destroyed. He led this band of Jews to begin the rebuilding of the Temple and the wall. (Ezra 3)

1. Matthew (Levi)
2. Mark (John)
3. John (brother of James)
4. Andrew
5. Bartholomew (Nathanael)
6. James (son of Zebedee)
7. James (son of Alphaeus)
8. Judas (called also Lebbaeus or Thaddaeus)
9. Judas Iscariot (replaced by Matthias)
10. Peter (Simon Peter)
11. Simon (Zelotes)
12. Thomas

Marys and Josephs

There are many people in the Bible to keep in order. It doesn't help when some of the important characters share the same names. Did you know that there are at least three Marys and Josephs?

Mary, mother of Jesus (Luke 1:26–2:20)
Mary Magdalene (John 20:1-2)
Mary and Martha (Luke 10:38-42; John 11)

Joseph, Old Testament: Joseph and his coat (Genesis 37)
Joseph, earthly father of Jesus (Luke 1:26–2:20)
Joseph of Arimethia (Matthew 27:57-60)

AKA: Throughout the Bible, various people experienced name changes. Here are just a few to note:
- Abram to Abraham (Genesis 17:5) • Sarai to Sarah (Genesis 17:15-16)
- Jacob to Israel (Genesis 32:28) • Simon to Peter (Matthew 16:18)
- Saul to Paul (Acts 13:9)

A Dozen Women You Need to Know...

Bathsheba	2 Samuel 11; 2 Samuel 12:24-25; 1 Kings 1:1
Delilah	Judges 16:4-31
Esther	Esther
Hagar	Genesis 21:8-21
Hannah	1 Samuel 1:1-2:21
Jezebel	1 Kings 19:1-3, 10; 1 Kings 21:1; 2 Kings 9:30-37
Lydia	Acts 16:11-15, 40
Miriam	Exodus 15:20-21; Numbers 12:1
Rebekah	Genesis 24:1; 25:19-28; 27
Ruth	Ruth
Salome	Mark 15:40; 16:1
Sarah	Genesis 18:9-15

Women Prophets (prophetess)

Only four women bear the title of "prophetess" in the Bible. (The reference in Isaiah 8:3 simply means the prophet's wife.)

Miriam	Exodus 15:20
Deborah	Judges 4:4
Huldah	2 Kings 22:14
Anna	Luke 2:36

Mephibosheth [mi-FIB-oh-sheth] – Mephibosheth was the son of Jonathan (King David's best friend). When Jonathan and Saul were in battle against David, the child's nurse grabbed Mephibosheth to flee to safety. However, she dropped him, leaving him lame. David took care of his friend's son for the rest of his life. (2 Samuel 4)

Prophets

There were numerous prophets mentioned in the Old Testament. Here are few whose Old Testament writings bear their names.

Isaiah	Ezekiel
Hosea	Zechariah
Jeremiah	Malachi
Micah	

What Is a Prophet?

The short answer is that a prophet is someone who speaks the word God wants shared with the people. The popular image of a prophet as someone who predicts the future is not completely accurate. A prophet is not a fortune teller, peering into a crystal ball or reading entrails, trying to perceive the particulars of what is about to happen.

However, a prophet does read the "signs of the times." The Old Testament prophets knew what was happening culturally and politically around them. Combining that awareness with an acute sensitivity to the will of God, the prophets often were able to say that if the people continued to live in the way they currently were, then such-and-such would happen.

They key to understanding the prophets is this sensitivity to the will of God. More than simply sharp observers of the life of their nations, the prophets were persons to whom God granted the ability to discern God's will for their time and place.

Mostly, the prophets called their people back from various forms of idolatry and immorality, warned them about God's judgment and

46

the consequences of continuing in their behavior, and offered God's amazing words of comfort when dire consequences did befall them.[2]

The Twelve Tribes of Israel

Jacob, son of Isaac, grandson of Abraham, had twelve sons. In Genesis 32, Jacob's name is changed to Israel. These twelve sons became the family lines upon which the tribes were based, each tracing its lineage back to one of the sons of Israel.

The sons, or tribes, are Reuben, Simeon, Levi, Judah, Issachar, Zebulun, Joseph, Benjamin, Dan, Naphtali, Gad, and Asher.

Jesus' Lineage

If Jesus is the Son of God, why is he called the son of David? Read Matthew 1:2-16 and Luke 3:23-38 to learn about the genealogy of Jesus. Matthew tells the genealogy of Joseph, and Luke tells the genealogy of Mary. (See also the discussion of the Lineage of Jesus in Chapter 5, pages 56–57.)

Nebuchadnezzar II [ne-buk-ud-NEZ-ur] was a ruler in Babylon from 605–562 B.C. He was responsible for throwing Shadrach, Meshach, and Abednego into the fiery furnace. But he wasn't all bad—he was also responsible for bringing them all out (Daniel 3)! He was also known for the construction of the Hanging Gardens of Babylon.

---

[1]Adapted from *Get Acquainted With Your Bible.* Copyright © 1993 Abingdon Press. Used by permission.
[2]Adapted from *Get Acquainted With Your Bible.* Copyright © 1993 Abingdon Press. Used by permission.

Key People in the Old Testament and When They Lived

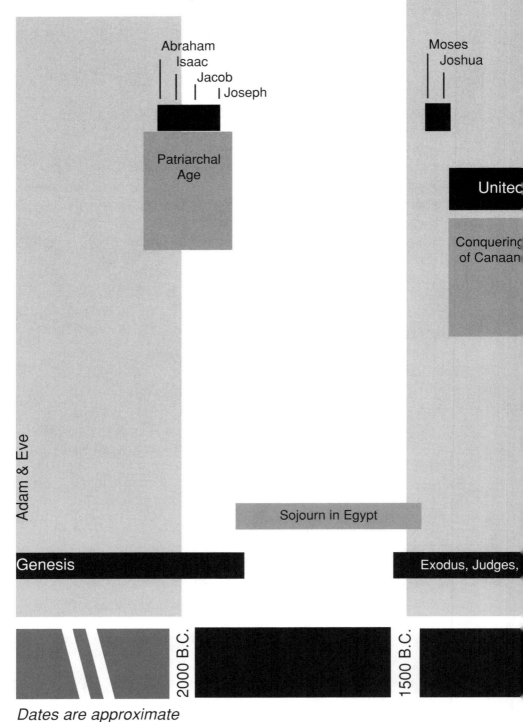

Abraham
Isaac
Jacob
Joseph

Moses
Joshua

Patriarchal Age

United

Conquering of Canaan

Adam & Eve

Sojourn in Egypt

Genesis

Exodus, Judges,

2000 B.C.

1500 B.C.

Dates are approximate

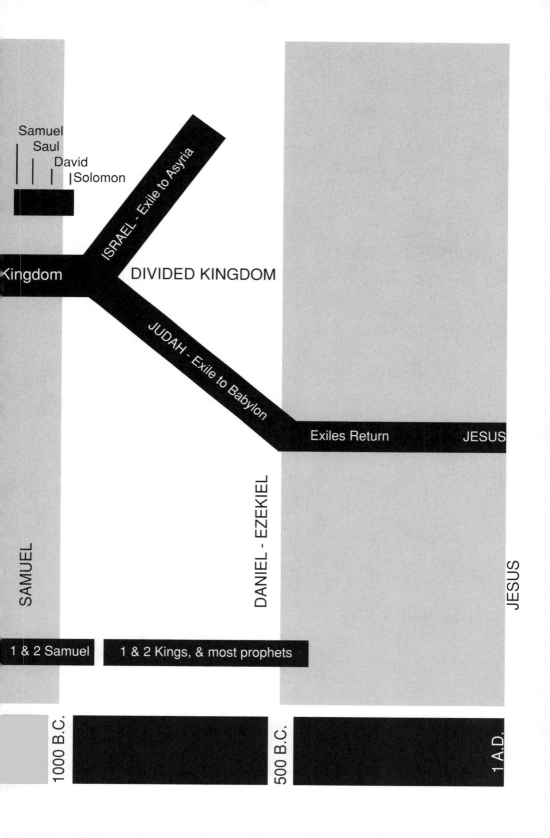

Chapter 5:
Jesus

Names for Jesus

In the previous chapter, we discussed names of God found in the Bible. The Bible also has many names for Jesus. Look up these verses and read about the Savior.

Alpha and Omega (Revelation 21:6)
Bread of Life (John 6:35)
Chief Cornerstone (Ephesians 2:20)
Chief Shepherd (1 Peter 5:4)
Good Shepherd (John 10:11)
Great Shepherd of the Sheep (Hebrews 13:20)
High Priest (Hebrews 3:1)
Holy One of God (Mark 1:24)
Immanuel, God with Us (Matthew 1:23)
King of Kings, Lord of Lords (Revelation 19:16)
Lamb of God (John 1:29)
Light of the World (John 9:5)
Lion of Judah (Revelation 5:5)
Lord of Glory (1 Corinthians 2:8)
Mediator between God and Men (1 Timothy 2:5)
Only Begotten of the Father (John 1:14)

Prophet (Acts 3:22)
Savior (Luke 1:47)
Seed of Abraham (Galatians 3:16)
Son of God (Mark 1:1)
Son of Man (Matthew 18:11)
The Word (John 1:1)

How Did Jesus Refer to Himself?

Look up these verses and learn about the great "I am."

I am the bread of life—John 6:35, 48
I am the light of the world—John 8:12; 9:5
I am the door—John 10:7
I am the good shepherd—John 10:11-14
I am the resurrection and the life—John 11:25
I am the way, the truth, and the life—John 14:6
I am the true vine—John 15:1, 5

Jesus Calls Himself God

Through the Gospels (Matthew, Mark, Luke, John), Jesus tries to help his followers understand who he is, what he is teaching, and what his relationship is to God. He uses many names and ways to describe himself to help them. Here are a few instances when Jesus calls himself God.

Matthew 12:8—"For the Son of Man is Lord of the sabbath."

Matthew 28:19—"Go therefore and make disciples of all nations, baptizing them in the name of the Father and of the Son and of the Holy Spirit."

Mark 2:5-12—"When Jesus saw their faith, he said to the paralytic, 'Son, your sins are forgiven.' Now some of the scribes were sitting there, questioning in their hearts, 'Why does this fellow speak in this way? It is blasphemy! Who can forgive sins but God alone?' At once Jesus perceived in his spirit that they were discussing these questions among themselves; and he said to them, 'Why do you raise such questions in your hearts? Which is easier, to say to the paralytic, "Your sins are forgiven," or to say, "Stand up and take your mat and walk"? But so that you may know that the Son of Man has authority on earth to forgive sins'—he said to the paralytic—'I say to you, stand up, take your mat and go to your home.' And he stood up, and immediately took the mat and went out before all of them; so that they were all amazed and glorified God, saying, 'We have never seen anything like this!' "

John 5:17-18—"But Jesus answered them, 'My Father is still working, and I also am working.' For this reason the Jews were seeking all the more to kill him, because he was not only breaking the sabbath, but was also calling God his own Father, thereby making himself equal to God."

John 8:58—"Jesus said to them, 'Very truly, I tell you, before Abraham was, I am.' "

John 10:30-33, 36-39—" 'The Father and I are one.' The Jews took up stones again to stone him. Jesus replied, 'I have shown you many good works from the Father. For which of these are you going to stone me?' The Jews answered, 'It is not for a good work that we are going to stone you, but for blasphemy, because you, though only a human being, are making yourself God.' can you say that the one whom the Father has sanctified and sent into the world is blaspheming because

I said, "I am God's Son"? If I am not doing the works of my Father, then do not believe me. But if I do them, even though you do not believe me, believe the works, so that you may know and understand that the Father is in me and I am in the Father.' Then they tried to arrest him again, but he escaped from their hands."

John 13:13-14—"You call me Teacher and Lord—and you are right, for that is what I am. So if I, your Lord and Teacher, have washed your feet, you also ought to wash one another's feet."

John 14:7-9—" 'If you know me, you will know my Father also. From now on you do know him and have seen him.' Philip said to him, 'Lord, show us the Father, and we will be satisfied.' Jesus said to him, 'Have I been with you all this time, Philip, and you still do not know me? Whoever has seen me has seen the Father. How can you say, 'Show us the Father'?"

Revelation 1:8—" 'I am the Alpha and the Omega,' says the Lord God, who is and who was and who is to come, the Almighty."

The Trinity

We know through the writings of the Old Testament that from the earliest times, the Hebrew faith believed in only one God. Jesus and his first followers, who were Jewish, also believed in just one God. Today, the Christian church also believes in one God but we describe our experience with God in more than one way. The early Christians sensed the presence of God with them in Jesus Christ. After Jesus died and rose again, they spoke of Jesus as the Son of God sent to them by God. Before his crucifixion, Jesus spoke to his followers about an advocate, or Holy Spirit, who would come to be with them after he was gone. The early Christians experienced God's presence with them through this Holy Spirit. Language for talking about our relationship with God expanded to three ways to experience God, but all the same, one God. Though the actual term *trinity* is not used in the Bible, this is how God as three-in-one has come to be understood.

God the Creator—God working to create the universe and everything in it

God the Son—Jesus, God walking the earth as a human being at a particular time and place

God the Holy Spirit—God present with us at this moment as a caring coach, comforter, and counselor[1]

God the Creator + God the Son + God the Holy Spirit = the Trinity

The Coming Messiah

The Old Testament has many verses known as *prophecies* that predict the coming of the "messiah," or "anointed one," a special person sent by God to atone for the sins of humankind. These passages are called Messianic prophecies.

Genesis 49:10—Says the Messiah will come from the tribe of Judah

Deuteronomy 18:15-18—God promises another prophet like Moses

Psalm 22—Predicts the crucifixion of Jesus

Isaiah 11:1-10—Nations will seek the counsel of Jesse's descendant

Isaiah 40:3—The Messiah will be preceded by a messenger

Isaiah 42:1-9—Describes Jesus' life

Isaiah 49:6—God's salvation will reach the ends of the earth

Isaiah 53 contains perhaps the most well-known Messianic prophecy:
    53:3—The Messiah will suffer and be rejected
    53:5—God's servant will be wounded and whipped
    53:7—God's servant will be silent before His accusers
    53:9—God's servant will be buried in a rich man's tomb
    53:12—God's servant will be crucified with criminals

Isaiah 61:1-2—Tells about the ministry of Jesus

Jeremiah 23:3-6—The Messiah will appear after the Jews return to Israel

Daniel 9:24-26—Daniel predicts when an anointed one will be rejected

Micah 5:2—The Messiah will be born in Bethlehem

Zechariah 9:9—The Messiah will enter Jerusalem while riding on a donkey

Zechariah 11:12-13—Prediction of the betrayal of Jesus for 30 pieces of silver

The Lineage of Jesus

The prophecies about the coming Messiah, recorded by Jewish prophets, expected a savior from the House of David. In both

Matthew 1:2-16 and Luke 3:23-38, the Gospel writers trace the lineage of Jesus through Mary and his earthly father, Joseph, back to David and even further back to the father of the Jewish nation, Abraham. While these two lists are not identical, each includes these well-known figures in Jesus' lineage:

King David (Matthew 1:6; Luke 3:31-32)
Jesse (Matthew 1:6; Luke 3:32)
Ruth and Boaz (Matthew 1:5; Luke 3:32)
Judah (Matthew 1:2-3; Luke 3:33-34)
Jacob (Matthew 1:16; Luke 3:34)
Isaac (Matthew 1:2; Luke 3:34)
Abraham (Matthew 1:2; Luke 3:34)

While Jesus Lived...

...the Roman Empire surrounded the entire Mediterranean Sea.

...Galilee and Judea were ruled by the Romans.

...the Great Wall of China had already been built.

...the Mayan civilization was developing in Central America.

...Buddhism was already five hundred years old in India.

...Tiberius succeeded Augustus as Roman emperor.

...there were two hundred million people throughout entire world.[2]

The Miracles of Jesus

The Old Testament documents many miracles performed by Jesus. Look up these Scripture references to read about a few:

Changing water into wine (John 2:1-12)
Healing of the royal official's son (John 4:46-54)
Healing of the Capernaum demoniac (Luke 4:31-37)
Catching a large number of fish (Luke 5:1-10; John 21:1-6)
Healing a leper (Matthew 8:1-3; Mark 1:40-45; Luke 5:12-15)
Healing a paralytic (Matthew 9:2-8; Mark 2:1-12; Luke 5:17-26)
Raising a widow's son (Luke 7:11-17)
Calming the stormy sea (Matthew 8:23-26; Mark 4:35-41;
        Luke 8:22-25)
Healing the Gerasene demoniac (Mark 5:1-20; Luke 8:26-39)
Healing a woman with internal bleeding (Matthew 9:20-22;
        Mark 5:25-34; Luke 8:43-48)
Feeding 5,000 men and their families (Matthew 14:13-21;
        Mark 6:30-44; Luke 9:10-17; John 6:1-14)
Walking on water (Matthew 14:22-33; Mark 6:45-51; John 6:16-21)
Healing a deaf man (Mark 7:31-37)
Healing a demoniac girl (Matthew 15:21-28; Mark 7:24-30)
Feeding the 4,000 men and their families (Matthew 15:32-39;
        Mark 8:1-9)
Healing a blind man (Mark 8:22-25; Mark 10:46-52; Luke 18:35-43)
Healing a man born blind (John 9:1-7)
Healing a demoniac boy (Matthew 17:14-21; Mark 9:14-29;
        Luke 9:37-43)
Healing 10 lepers (Luke 17:11-19)
Raising of Lazarus (John 11:1-44)

Chronology of Jesus' Life and Ministry in Scripture

- Birth (Luke 2:6-7)

- Jesus, at age 12, stays in Jerusalem to attend the temple court and learn from the teachers there (Luke 2:41-52)

- Baptized (Matthew 3:13-17; Mark 1:9-11; Luke 3:21-22)

- Temptation (Matthew 4:1-11)

- Begins preaching (Matthew 4:12-17)

- Performs first miracle (John 2:1-12)

- Calls his first disciples (Matthew 4:18-22)

- Delivers the Sermon on the Mount (Matthew 5; Luke 6:20-49)

- Walks on water (Matthew 14:22-33; Mark 6:45-52; John 6:15-21)

- Drives the money changers out of the Temple (Matthew 21:12-13; Luke 19:45-46)

- The Last Supper (Matthew 26:26-30; Mark 14:22-25; Luke 22:17-20)

- Prays in the garden (Matthew 26:36-46; Mark 14:32-42; Luke 22:39-46)

- Stands trial (Matthew 27:1-32; Mark 15:1-22; Luke 23:1-32; John 18:28-40; 19:1-16)

- Crucifixion (Matthew 27:33-56; Mark 15:22-41; Luke 23:33-49; John 19:17-30)

- Resurrection (John 20:19-29)

Pilgrimages, Feasts, and Festivals That Jesus Observed

Shabbat (the sabbath), according to Jewish law, is observed on Saturday and is a day of rest. During biblical times, it was very important under Jewish law to refrain from work, travel, or any activity on the sabbath. Jesus kept the sabbath but taught that the needs of people came before the letter of the law. (Matthew 12:10-12)

Remember the sabbath day, and keep it holy. Six days you shall labor and do all your work. But the seventh day is a sabbath to the Lord your God; you shall not do any work. (Exodus 20:8-10)

A man was there with a withered hand, and they asked him, "Is it lawful to cure on the sabbath?" so that they might accuse him. He said to them, "Suppose one of you has only one sheep and it falls into a pit on the sabbath; will you not lay hold of it and lift it out? How much more valuable is a human being than a sheep! So it is lawful to do good on the sabbath." (Matthew 12:10-12)

Rosh Hashanah (The New Year) means "beginning of the year." During Rosh Hashanah, the *shofar*, or ram's horn, trumpet sounds during the special synagogue service. The theme of the festival is repentance, and families often celebrate with extensive meals at home.

On the first day of the seventh month you shall have a holy convocation; you shall not work at your occupations. It is a day for you to blow the trumpets. (Numbers 29:1)

Yom Kippur (Day of Atonement) begins eight days after Rosh Hashanah and is a day to confess and repent of wrongdoing.

This shall be a statute to you forever: In the seventh month, on the tenth day of the month, you shall deny yourselves, and shall do no work, neither the citizen nor the alien who resides among you. For on this day atonement shall be made for you, to cleanse you; from all your sins you shall be clean before the Lord. (Leviticus 16:29-30)

Sukkot (Feast of Tabernacles) commemorates the Exodus from Egypt. With a theme of thanks for the harvest, Jewish people today often build outdoor booths for meals and time with family. It begins five days after Yom Kippur and is one of the three major pilgrimage festivals where all the Jews who could traveled to the Temple in Jerusalem. (Leviticus 23:33-43)

In the Gospel of John, chapter 7, Jesus is reported as expected to go to the feast in Jerusalem with his family:

After this, Jesus went around in Galilee, purposely staying away from Judea because the Jews there were waiting to take his life. But when the Jewish Feast of Tabernacles was near, Jesus' brothers said to him, "You ought to leave here and go to Judea, so that your disciples may see the miracles you do." (John 7:1-3, NIV)

Passover (Unleavened Bread), another pilgrimage feast, celebrates the liberation of the Israelites from slavery in Egypt. The seder meal, with special prayers and rituals, is a significant part of the holiday. Jesus' last meal with his disciples, or "The Last Supper," may have been a Passover seder.

You shall keep the festival of unleavened bread. Seven days you shall eat unleavened bread, as I commanded you, at the time appointed in the month ... you came out from Egypt. (Exodus 34:18)

Now the Passover of the Jews was near, and many went up from the country to Jerusalem before the Passover to purify themselves. They were looking for Jesus and were asking one another as they stood in the temple, "What do you think? Surely he will not come to the festival, will he?" (John 11:55-56)

How is the day to celebrate Easter determined?

For almost 300 years, Christians couldn't decide among themselves. Then, in A.D. 325 at the First Council of Nicaea, it was decided that a common date was needed. First decided was that Easter would be celebrated on Sunday since that is the day that it was traditionally believed that Jesus was resurrected. Then lots of different people came up with theories, and it wasn't until the creation of the Gregorian calendar in 1582 that the method came into practice that is still used today. Basically, Easter is the first Sunday after the 14th day of the lunar month that falls on or after March 21 (the day of the vernal equinox).

Shavuot (Pentecost) is the last of the three pilgrimage festivals, is seven weeks after Passover. In the Bible, it is called the festival of weeks or in Hebrew, *Shavuot*, because it counted in the number of weeks from Passover. It celebrates the peak of the season for barley and wheat and the first ripening of fruit.

In John 5:1, the festival going on when Jesus healed the lame man is thought to be Shavuot.

After this there was a festival of the Jews, and Jesus went up to Jerusalem. Now in Jerusalem by the Sheep Gate there is a pool, called in Hebrew Beth-zatha, which has five porticoes. In these lay many in-valids—blind, lame, and paralyzed. One man was there who had been ill for thirty-eight years. When Jesus saw him lying there and knew that he had been there a long time, he said to him, "Do you want to be made well?" (John 5:1-6)

---

[1]Adapted from *Get Acquainted With Your Bible.* Copyright © 1993 Abingdon Press. Used by permission.
[2]Adapted from *Get Acquainted With Your Bible.* Copyright © 1993 Abingdon Press. Used by permission.

MEDITERRANEAN
AREA TODAY

SCALE OF MILES

0 50 100   200   300

Chapter 6:
Biblical Geography

We have a tendency to envision ancient cities as they are described in biblical stories. However, as our everyday surroundings change with the times, so do the biblical cities. For example, today many biblical cities are located in Turkey; and although they maintain their heritage, they have developed into modern cities and, despite political unrest, popular tourist destinations.

Bethlehem, with a current population of nearly 22,000, is controlled by the Palestinian Authority.[1]

Nazareth, during the time Jesus lived there, had a population of less than 200. Today, more than 60,000 Israeli Arabs live there, and Upper Nazareth is home to thousands more Jewish residents.

Tarsus, the city where the Apostle Paul was born, today is an affluent agricultural and cotton-milling center with a population of 216,382. In Paul's day, the city was actually a seaport, but because of centuries of silting, it is now about 12 miles off the coast of the Mediterranean Sea.[2]

Jerusalem is a modern metropolis of 693,200 people.

Praslin, Seychelles is often called the original Garden of Eden.

▶ *FAST FACT:* Mark Antony and Cleopatra first met in Tarsus during the 1st century B.C.[3]

▶ *FAST FACT:* Turkey lies in two continents: Asia and Europe. The Asian portion of Turkey is about the size of Texas; the European portion is about the size of Massachusetts.

Power Walking
Read Act 1:12, "Then they returned to Jerusalem from the hill called the Mount of Olives, a sabbath day's walk from the city" (NIV).[4]

What Is a Sabbath-day's Journey?
According to Jewish tradition, it was the distance a person could travel without violating the law. Bible scholars believe that distance to be about 3/4 of a mile.

How does a Sabbath-day's journey compare to another day's journey? It has been said that Paul typically walked about 13 miles a day.[5]

Famous Places in the Old Testament

Babel [BAY-buhl]: City in Plain of Shinar. Site of tower built in Genesis 11:1. Tower was possibly a ziggurat, a stepped tower with a temple on top.

Babylonia [bab-uh-LOH-nee-uh]: A region of west Asia at east end of Fertile Crescent. Babylon was capital. King Nebuchadnezzar of Babylonia took Jerusalem twice and destroyed it (2 Kings 14:1-25). The Jews were in exile there for forty-eight years (586–538 B.C.).

Sidon

Tyre

PHOENICIA

ABILENE

MT. HERMON

Caesarea
Philippi

PANEAS

ITURAEA

TRACHONITIS

Lake Semechonitis

ULATHA

GALILEE

Capernaum

Sea of Galilee

Bethsaida
Julias

GAULANITIS

BATANAEA

AURANITIS

Cana
Nazareth

MT. TABOR

MT. CARMEL

DECAPOLIS

Mediterranean Sea

Caesarea

MT. GERIZIM

SAMARIA

PEREA

Joppa

Jericho

JERUSALEM

Bethlehem

Bethany

Gaza

JUDEA

Lake Asphaltitis
(Dead Sea)

IDUMEA

N A B A T A E A

N

W   E

S

**PALESTINE
AT THE TIME
OF JESUS**

SCALE OF MILES

0 5 10 15 20 25 30

ICN 235103

THE
KINGDOMS
OF ISRAEL
AND JUDAH

SCALE OF MILES
0   10   20   30   40

• Damascus

Sidon •

KINGDOM OF
DAMASCUS
(Syria)

Tyre •   Dan •

PHOENICIA

ISRAEL

SAMARIA •

River Jordan

The
Great
Sea

Joppa •

Bethel •   Jericho •

JERUSALEM •
Tokea •
Moresheth •

AMMON

Gaza •

PHILISTIA

Lake Asphaltitis
(Dead Sea)

JUDAH

Beersheba •

MOAB

Arabian Desert

Kadesh-
barnea •

EDOM

N

KINGDOM OF
EGYPT

W   E

Elath •

S

ICN 235170

68

Bethel [BETH-uhl]: A town of Palestine, eleven miles north of Jerusalem, originally called Luz.

Canaan [KAY-nuhn]: Old name of Palestine. Inhabited by Canaanites before Hebrew conquest. Known as the Promised Land.

Damascus [duh-MAS-kuhs]: City in Syria on a plateau watered by the rivers Abana and Pharpar. Captured by David (2 Samuel 8:5-6). Paul was converted on his way to this city to persecute Christians (Acts 9:1-9).

Eden [EE-duhn]: A country where God planted a garden for Adam to till and keep (Genesis 2:8-17).

Egypt [EE-jipt]: Country watered by the Nile River from the Mediterranean to the First Cataract. Upper Egypt included the river valley. Lower Egypt consisted of the delta region. Ruled by pharaohs. Egypt played an important part in several eras of biblical history, including the enslavement of the Hebrew people.

Gomorrah [guh-MOR-uh]: City in plain of the Jordan River destroyed by fire from heaven because of the wickedness of its inhabitants (Genesis 18:16-33; 19:12-29).

Jericho [JER-uh-koh]: City in valley of Jordan, near the northern end of the Dead Sea. Oldest settlement in Palestine. First city to fall to the Hebrews during the conquest (Joshua 6:1).

Kadesh-Barnea [kay-dish-BAHR-nee-uh]: Place at which the Israelites were sent to wander in the wilderness for 40 years.

Palestine [PAL-uh-stine]: Land in southwest corner of Asia area bordered by Kadesh-Barnea on south, Mount Hermon on north, Mediterranean Sea on west, and desert on east. Also known as the Promised Land or the Holy Land.

Sodom [SOD-uhm]: One of five cities in plain of Jordan, notorious for its wickedness. Lot and his daughters were spared from its destruction (Genesis 19:12-29).

Syria [SIHR-ee-uh]: Country on east coast of Mediterranean and extending inland, north and east of Israel. Antioch was capital. Damascus was also in Syria.

Ur: City of Babylonia on the west bank of the Euphrates. An ancient city of Sumer later occupied by the Chaldeans. Birthplace of Abraham (Genesis 11:27-31).

Famous Places in the New Testament

Athens [ATH-inz]: Capital of Attica, one of the Greek states. Center of enlightenment in science, literature, and art for ancient world. Paul preached there with little success (Acts 17:16-34).

Bethlehem [BETH-li-him]: Town in the hill country of Judah, five miles south of Jerusalem. Rachel was buried near there (Genesis 35:19). Home of Naomi, Ruth, and Boaz. David came from Bethlehem, and it was expected that the Messiah would be born there (Micah 5:2). Joseph and Mary went there to be registered at the time of Jesus' birth.

Calvary [KAL-vuh-ree]: Place just outside the walls of Jerusalem where Jesus was crucified.

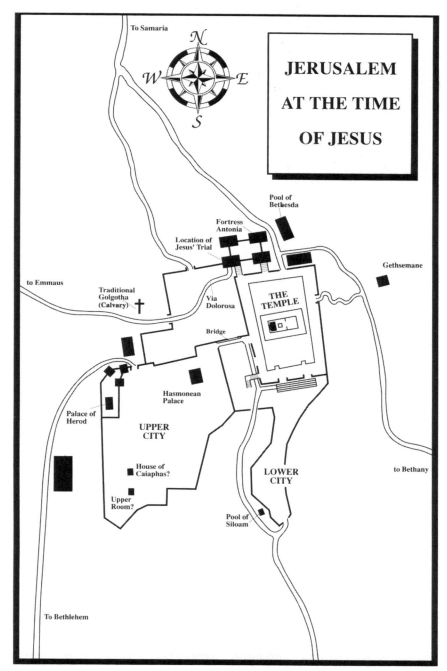

JERUSALEM AT THE TIME OF JESUS

To Samaria

N
W E
S

Pool of Bethesda

Fortress Antonia

Location of Jesus' Trial

to Emmaus

Traditional Golgotha (Calvary)

Via Dolorosa

THE TEMPLE

Gethsemane

Bridge

Hasmonean Palace

Palace of Herod

UPPER CITY

House of Caiaphas?

Upper Room?

LOWER CITY

to Bethany

Pool of Siloam

To Bethlehem

Adapted from *Tear-off Bible Map Series*, Copyright © 1994 by Abingdon Press.

THE

MINISTRY

OF JESUS

Later Ministry
of Jesus

SCALE OF MILES

0 5 10 15 20 25 30

Sidon

Mt. Hermon

Sarepta

Tyre

Caesarea Philippi

Gischala

Capernaum

Bethsaida-Julias

Magadan

SEA OF GALILEE

GALILEE

Nazareth

Mt. Tabor

Abila

Gadara

Caesarea

Ginae

SAMARIA

Emmaeus

GALILEAN MINISTRY

Capernaum

Bethsaida-Julias

Cana

Gennesaret

Nazareth

Magadan

SEA OF
GALILEE

Nain

Bethel

Ephraim

Philadelphia

JERUSALEM

Jericho

Bethany

Bethlehem

Dead Sea

N

W   E

S

JUDEA

ICN 23512X

72

Emmaus [i-MAY-uhs]: A village about seven miles northwest of Jerusalem. Two disciples met Jesus on the road to this town following his resurrection (Luke 24:13-35).

Galilee [GAL-uh-lee]: Northern region of Palestine. Separated from Judea by Samaria. Nazareth, home of Jesus, was there.

Jerusalem [ji-ROO-suh-luhm]: City chosen by David as his capital. Located on a tableland on the crest of the central ridge of Palestine. Site of the Temple. Known as Zion. Destroyed by the Babylonians in 587/86 B.C. and again by the Romans in A.D. 70.

Nazareth [NAZ-uh-rith]: Town in lower Galilee where Mary and Joseph lived and where Jesus was brought up (Matthew 2:23; Luke 2:39-40). The townspeople rejected Jesus when he announced his mission (Luke 4:16-30).

Patmos [PAT-muhs]: Small island of the southwest coast of Asia Minor. John was banished to this island because of his witness to Christ. There he wrote the Book of Revelation (Revelation 1:9).

Tarsus [TAHR-suhs]: Chief city of Cilicia in eastern Asia Minor. Birthplace of Paul and a great commercial center (Acts 21:39).

▶ *FAST FACT:* **Bethel** [BETH-uhl]: A town of Palestine, 11 miles north of Jerusalem, is mentioned more than any other biblical town except Jerusalem.

Famous Places in the New Testament Stories of the Early Church

Antioch [AN-tee-ok]: (1) City in Syria located on banks of Orontes River. Disciples first called Christians there (Acts 11:19-26). Church sent Paul and Barnabas on first missionary journey (Acts 13:1-3). (2) Town in Asia Minor known as Pisidian Antioch. Visited by Paul and Barnabas on first missionary journey (Acts 13:13-52).

Colossae [kuh-LOS-ee]: City of southwest Phrygia in Asia Minor. A Christian community grew there under the leadership of Epaphras and later of Archippus (Colossians 1:7; Philemon 1:2). Philemon was a member of this church, as was Onesimus (Colossians 4:9).

Corinth [KOR-inth]: City of Greece on isthmus between Peloponnesus and mainland. Paul founded church there on second missionary journey (Acts 18:1-17).

Galatia [guh-LAY-shuh]: Roman province in central Asia Minor. Paul visited the area on his missionary journey (Acts 16:6; 18:23).

Thessalonica [thes-uh-luh-NIGH-kuh]: Capital of a district of Macedonia, this city was located on the Gulf of Salonika. On the Via Egnatia, it was visited by Paul (Acts 17:1-9); and he wrote two letters to the Christians there.

Four Famous Bodies of Water

Dead Sea: the lowest sea in the world. It is 1,300 feet below sea level. No water flows out of it and no plants or fish can live in the salty water. It is also called the Salt Sea (Genesis 14:3).

Jordan [JOR-duhn]: means the descender. Israel's longest river, and most important river of Palestine. It rises close to Mount Hermon in the north and flows into the Sea of Galilee. It flows over 200 miles through the Jordan Valley from Baniyas, ancient Caesarea Philippi, before flowing into the southern tip of Dead Sea.

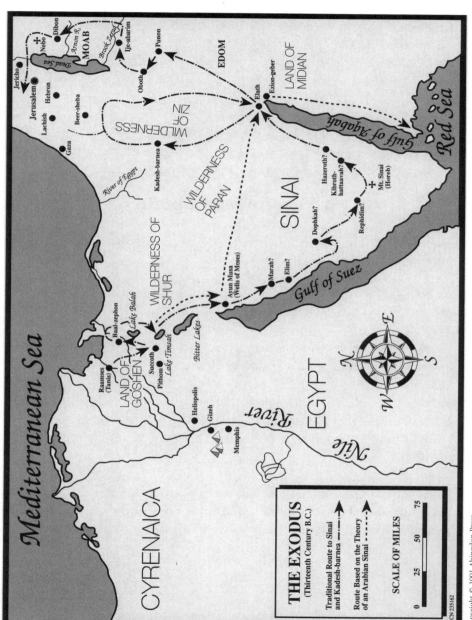

THE EXODUS
(Thirteenth Century B.C.)

Traditional Route to Sinai
and Kadesh-barnea ·—·—·►

Route Based on the Theory
of an Arabian Sinai ·····►

SCALE OF MILES

0   25   50   75

Mediterranean Sea

CYRENAICA

EGYPT

Nile River

Memphis

Gizeh

Heliopolis

Raamses (Tanis)

LAND OF GOSHEN

Pithom

Succoth

Baal-zephon

Lake Balah

Lake Timsah

Bitter Lakes

WILDERNESS OF SHUR

Gulf of Suez

Ayun Musa (Wells of Moses)

Marah?

Elim?

Dophkah?

Rephidim?

Mt. Sinai (Horeb)

Kibroth-hattaavah?

Hazeroth?

SINAI

WILDERNESS OF PARAN

Kadesh-barnea

River of Egypt

Gaza

Lachish

Beer-sheba

Hebron

Jerusalem

Jericho

Nebo

Dibon

MOAB

Arnon R.

Brook Zered

Ije-abarim

Oboth

Punon

Dead Sea

WILDERNESS OF ZIN

EDOM

Elath

Ezion-geber

LAND OF MIDIAN

Gulf of Aqabah

Red Sea

IGN 235162

Red Sea: also known as the "sea of reeds," sea on eastern side of North Africa opening into the Indian Ocean. Northern end divides into Gulf of Suez and Gulf of Akabah, forming Sinai Peninsula. Hebrews crossed this sea on dry land to escape the Egyptians (Exodus 14:1).

Sea of Galilee: also known as the **Sea of Tiberias** (John 6:1) and the **Lake of Gennesaret** (Luke 5:1). Jesus spoke to a crowd from a boat on the Sea of Galilee. It is about 12 miles long and 7 miles wide.

Five Famous Mountains

Horeb [HOR-eb]: the mountain of God in the Sinai peninsula, also known as Mount Sinai (Exodus 17:1-7).

Nebo [NEE-boh]: mountain in Moab opposite Jericho from which Moses viewed the Promised Land (Deuteronomy 34:1-5).

Sinai [SIGH-nigh]: the mountain of God in the Sinai peninsula, also known as Mount Horeb (Exodus 19:20).

Tabor [TAY-buhr]: mountain at northeast end of Valley of Jezreel near Nazareth. The Israelite forces assembled there before fighting Sisera (Judges 4:4-7). Thought to be the site of the Transfiguration (Luke 9:28-36).

Zion [ZIGH-uhn]: one of the hills on which Jerusalem stands. After Temple built on Mount Moriah and ark transferred to it, the name Zion was extended to the entire city (2 Kings 19:21).

---

[1]"Bethlehem"; http://www.bibleplaces.com/bethlehem.htm.

[2]"Tarsus," *Encycopædia Britannica* online (Encyclopædia Britannica, Inc., 2008); www.britannica.com/eb/article-9071333/Tarsus#248112.hook.

[3]"Tarsus," *Encycopædia Britannica* online.

[4]Reference to "Acts 1:12 (NIV)"; http://www.biblegateway.com/passage/?search =acts%201:12.

[5]Reference to "Journey"; http://www.biblegateway.com/resources/dictionaries/dict_ meaning.php?source=1&wid=T0002119.

Chapter 7:
Topics the Bible
Doesn't Ignore

What do you bring to the Bible? Your humanity. Everything you have ever thought, done, experienced, or agonized over can be dealt with by the Bible. Every human emotion is expressed there.

What does the Bible bring to you? God's authoritative guidance and counsel. The Bible has to express humanity in order to reach us; it has to express divinity in order to save us.[1]

The wisdom of the Bible, though recorded thousands of years ago, speaks to us today on topics like family, love, sorrow, forgiveness, and hope. Some passages are very specific. As you read, take care when isolating one verse from others. Read the verses just before and after it. As you read, ask yourself who is speaking, who the audience is, and what the setting is. Looking for the context of the verse will continue to add to your understanding each time you read the Bible for devotion, inspiration, and study.

While the Bible covers many, many topics across centuries, the over-riding message remains the story of God's love for us. From Genesis through the New Testament books, you will see again and again God's love, God's promises and forgiveness for people. In Mark, Jesus gives his greatest two commandments to us, to return that love to God and to each other:

" 'You shall love the Lord your God with all your heart, and with all your soul, and with all your mind, and with all your strength.' The second is this, 'You shall love your neighbor as yourself.' There is no other commandment greater than these." (Mark 12:30-31)

Depression

Many people in the Bible suffered bouts of depression.
- Abraham (Genesis 15)
- Jonah (Jonah 4)
- Job (Book of Job)
- Elijah (1 Kings 19)
- King Saul (1 Samuel 16:14-23)
- Jeremiah (Book of Jeremiah)
- David (Psalms)

▶ *FAST FACT:* The Book of Psalms is widely known as a record book of praise and the source of so many hymns. However, 50 out of the 150 psalms are psalms of lament, deeply emotional words of grief, sorrow, and sometimes anger. Here are just a few of these: Psalms 6; 31; 34; 40; 51; 55; 69; 77; 86; 107; 116; 130; 143.

Do you think Adam and Eve experienced depression after they sinned against God? King David certainly did. "I am utterly bowed down and prostrate; all day long I go around mourning.... / I am utterly spent and crushed; I groan because of the tumult of my heart." (Psalm 38:6, 8)

"Why are you cast down, O my soul, and why are you disquieted within me? / Hope in God; for I shall again praise him, my help.... / For you are the God in whom I take refuge." (Psalm 42:5; 43:2)

The Bible speaks about...Anxiety
Luke 12:22-34; Philippians 4:4-9

The Bible speaks about...Fear
Isaiah 51:7-16; John 14

The Bible speaks about...Joy
Isaiah 12; Luke 15; Galatians 5:13-26; James 1:2-18; 1 Peter 4:12-19

The Patience of Job—*why was he so patient?*

One day a messenger came to Job to tell him that the Sabeans killed his servants and the oxen and donkeys that they were watching. Then, another messenger told him that fire came down and burned up his sheep and those servants. Up came the third messenger to inform Job that the Chaldeans took his camels and those servants. Then came the fourth messenger to tell Job that a great wind came up, knocked down his house and killed his sons and daughters. So, in one day he lost his children, his house, his servants, and all his livestock. In the end, though, Job realized God's sovereignty and repented of his doubts and anger. The last part of Job 42 tells us that God gave Job back more than twice as much as he had before. He ended up with 14,000 sheep, 6,000 camels, 1,000 yoke of oxen, 1,000 donkeys, 7 sons, and 3 daughters (and they were the most beautiful women in the land). Job lived to see four generations.

Eating Disorders and Body Image

What does the Bible say about eating disorders and body image? While the Bible doesn't specifically use those terms, it does talk about respect for our bodies and the wondrous way we were made. See Psalm 139:13-16:

"For it was you who formed my inward parts; you knit me together in my mother's womb. / I praise you, for I am fearfully and wonderfully made. Wonderful are your works; / that I know very well. My frame was not hidden from you, when I was being made in secret, intricately woven in the depths of the earth. / Your eyes beheld my unformed substance. / In your book were written all the days that were formed for me, when none of them as yet existed."

Look also at Romans 12:1: "Present your bodies as a living sacrifice, holy and acceptable to God, which is your spiritual worship."

And 1 Corinthians 6:19-20: "Do you not know that your body is a temple of the Holy Spirit within you, which you have from God, and that you are not your own? For you were bought with a price; therefore glorify God in your body."

Jesus understands pain, and he wants people to heal.

Grief

"Weeping may linger for the night, but joy comes with the morning.... / You have turned my mourning into dancing; you have taken off my sackcloth and clothed me with joy, / so that my soul may praise you and not be silent. O LORD my God, I will give thanks to you forever." (Psalm 30:5b, 11-12)

In our fast-paced society, the common human emotion of grief has become somewhat overlooked and sometimes even looked down upon. Oftentimes, people want to ignore the emotion in themselves and in others. However, the Bible tells us that grief is a normal process.

Read Genesis 37 about Jacob and his love for his son Joseph. How did Jacob react to the loss of Joseph? How did Jacob's family react?

There are many examples of sorrow, mourning, and grief in the Bible. Deuteronomy 34:8 says, "The Israelites wept for Moses in the plains of Moab for thirty days; then the period of mourning for Moses was ended." An important message in this verse is that the period of mourning *ended.*

The Bible speaks about...Hope
Romans 5:1-11; Colossians 1:3-27

The Bible speaks about...Death
Luke 12:13-21; 1 Corinthians 15

The Bible speaks about...Comfort
Psalm 23; Psalm 46; Romans 8:18-39; John 14:1-4, 15-27; 2 Corinthians 1:3-7

Caring for Each Other

What does the Bible say about helping others?

Read the story of the good Samaritan (Luke 10:25-37). "You shall love the Lord your God with all your heart, and with all your soul, and with all your strength, and with all your mind; and your neighbor as yourself" (verse 27). What does this parable say about the way we care for others?

When we are helping our neighbors, who are we really helping? Read Matthew 25:35-36, 40: " 'I was hungry and you gave me food, I was thirsty and you gave me something to drink, I was a stranger and you welcomed me, I was naked and you gave me clothing, I was sick and you took care of me, I was in prison and you visited me.' ... 'Truly I tell you, just as you did it to one of the least of these who are members of my family, you did it to me.' "

"The one who sows sparingly will also reap sparingly, and the one who sows bountifully will also reap bountifully. Each of you must give as you have made up your mind, not reluctantly or under compulsion, for God loves a cheerful giver. And God is able to provide you with every blessing in abundance, so that by always having enough of everything, you may share abundantly in every good work." (2 Corinthians 9:6-8)

The Bible speaks about...Compassion
Jonah 3; John 11:17-44; 1 John 3:11-24

The Bible speaks about...Friendship
Proverbs 27:6, 10, 17; Ecclesiastes 4:7-12; John 11:1-44

The Bible speaks about...Love
Mark 12:28-34; 1 Corinthians 13; Galatians 5:13-26; 1 John 4:7-21

Heaven

We do not know a lot about heaven and what it is like. Jesus said to his followers, "In my Father's house there are many dwelling places. If it were not so, would I have told you that I go to prepare a place for you?" (John 14:2). The followers of Jesus then and now expect to reunite with Jesus in a place he has prepared for them one day.

These New Testament Scriptures tell us that heaven is eternal and that treasures and success on earth are less permanent than treasure in heaven earned by people who know how to live through Christ.

"For we know that if the earthly tent we live in is destroyed, we have a building from God, a house not made with hands, eternal in the heavens." (2 Corinthians 5:1)

"But store up for yourselves treasures in heaven, where neither moth nor rust consumes and where thieves do not break in and steal." (Matthew 6:20)

We do know a little about what *isn't* in heaven from the Book of Revelation:

21:1—*no sea*—There will be no chaotic force of "uncreation," which is the opposite of God's being and creating, loose in the world.

21:4—*no tears, death, sorrow, crying, pain*—Life will be abundantly full.

21:18—*no persons who are cowardly, faithless, or impure; no murderers, fornicators, sorcerers, idolators, or liars*—the city that is filled with God's presence will be freed and empty of the sins that infect the present world. (Note that these sins were specifically those found either in the pagan cults and the emperor worship that surrounded the late first-century Christians or in the actions of former Christians who renounced their faith out of fear of persecution.)

21:22—*no temple*—The entire city is holy with God's immediate presence.

21:23, 25; 22:5—*no sun, moon, night, or closed gates*—God is light. Therefore, there is no darkness nor any of the fears or anxieties associated with the darkness.

22:3—*no curse*—The curse pronounced on the occasion of the first sin (Genesis 3:17) will be no more.[2]

Anger

"Let everyone be ... slow to anger; for your anger does not produce God's righteousness." (James 1:19-20)

Have you read the story of Jonah? I mean the part *after* he was swallowed by the fish. He became very angry when the Lord didn't destroy Nineveh. Read about it in Jonah chapters 3 and 4.

Anger creeps into everyone's life. Even Jesus experienced anger (read Mark 3:5). However, it is not an emotion that God wants people to nurture. Read what Jesus says about anger in Matthew 5:21-26. What is an angry person liable to? What does speaking out in anger make us liable to?

The Bible speaks about...Bitterness
James 3:13-18; Ephesians 4:29-32

The Bible speaks about...Peace
John 14:25-27; Ephesians 2:14-18; Philippians 4:4-9; Isaiah 9:1-7; Psalm 34:11-14; Colossians 3:15; 1 Peter 3:8-12

The Bible speaks about...Revenge
Matthew 5:38-47; Romans 12:17-21

The Bible speaks about...Eternal Life
1 John 5:1-15; Romans 6:15-23; John 3:1-21

Racism

The Old Testament documents racism (Leviticus 25:44-46) as does the New Testament (Luke 10:30-37). Today, on every continent and in every country there is racism. A group of people believing that they are better than other groups is evidence of people turning away from God the Creator (Job 31:13-15; Proverbs 22:2).

Even though slavery and class distinction were common practices in biblical times, God warned God's chosen people not to oppress people of other races (Exodus 22:21; 23:9). And Jesus was fair to all people: "So they sent their disciples to him ... saying, 'Teacher, we know that you are sincere, and teach the way of God in accordance with truth, and show deference to no one; for you do not regard people with partiality' " (Matthew 22:16). Through Christ, we are all one— there is no differentiation in skin color or socio-economic class.

"For in Christ Jesus you are all children of God through faith. As many of you as were baptized into Christ have clothed yourselves with Christ. There is no longer Jew or Greek, there is no longer slave or free, there is no longer male and female; for all of you are one in Christ Jesus." (Galatians 3:26-28)

The Bible speaks about...Forgiveness
Psalm 130; Matthew 18:21-35; Colossians 2:6-15; Luke 23:26-49

The Bible speaks about...Sin
Genesis 3; Psalm 32; 51; Romans 3:23-24; 1 John 1:5-2:14; John 3:17-21

The Bible speaks about...Temptation
James 1:13-18; Ephesians 6:10-20; 1 Corinthians 10:12-13

The Bible speaks about...Adultery
Matthew 5:27; Galatians 5:13-26

The Bible speaks about...Marriage

Genesis 2:18-25; Ephesians 5:22-33

The Bible speaks about...Relationships

Ephesians 4:25-26; 6:1-9; John 15: 12-13; Ecclesiastes 4:9-10; Romans 12:9-16

Going Green

In the very first chapter of the Bible, we read about God's creative hand as God made the heavens and the earth, the water and the land, and living creatures to inhabit it all. In verse 26, God gives humankind ruling power over the fish of the sea, the birds of the air, the cattle, "and over all the wild animals of the earth, and over every creeping thing that creeps upon the earth." God gave us plants and trees and saw that it was good (Genesis 1:11-12).

God gave us many wonderful gifts, one of which is nature. God provided a way for humankind to receive joy and sustenance from nature and entrusted the continuation of God's beautiful creation to humankind.

"In his hands are the depths of the earth; the heights of the mountains are his also. The sea is his, for he made it, and the dry land, which his hands have formed." (Psalm 95:4-5)

---

[1]Adapted from DISCIPLE: BECOMING DISCIPLES THROUGH BIBLE STUDY, Study Manual, Second Edition (Abingdon, 1993); p. 10. Used by permission.

[2]Adapted from *Get Acquainted With Your Bible.* Copyright © 1993 Abingdon Press. Used by permission.

Chapter 8:
Based on the Bible

The Bible is the most influential book written. Every day in routine conversations we hear Bible references; and many times we don't even think about the words, phrases, and concepts as being from the Bible. On the other hand, some figures of speech that have worked their way into our conversations that we think are from the Bible, really are not.

Sayings that are *not* in the Bible	See what the Bible *really* says
Money is the root of all evil.	Timothy 6:10
Cleanliness is next to godliness.	Psalm 24:4-6
The things I once hated I now love, and the things I loved I now hate.	1 Corinthians 13:11
Spare the rod and spoil the child.	Proverbs 23:13
God helps those who help themselves.	Psalm 72:12
Moderation in all things.	1 Corinthians 9:25

The lion shall lay down with the lamb.   Isaiah 11:6; 65:25

Pride comes before the fall.   Proverbs 16:18

Seven deadly sins—gluttony, greed,
sloth, lust, vanity, envy, wrath   Proverbs 6:16-19

Sweat of your brow   Genesis 3:19

"The writing's on the wall"—This famous phrase has its roots in the Book of Daniel. As King Belshazzar was hosting a great feast, he and his guests began praising the gods of gold, silver, bronze, iron, wood, and stone. Immediately the fingers of human hands appeared and began writing on the wall of the palace. The king saw this and, needless to say, it scared him. He called all his advisors together but no one could tell him what the words meant or even what they were.

Finally, someone told him about Daniel who had interpreted dreams for Belshazzar's father, Nebuchadnezzar II. Daniel came in and told him the words were *MENE* (God has numbered the days of your kingdom and is bringing it to an end), *TEKEL* (God has weighed you on the scales and you have been found wanting), and *PERES* (your kingdom is divided and given to the Medes and Persians). Belshazzar promoted Daniel and made a proclamation to the nation about Daniel's importance. That very night Belshazzar was killed. (Daniel 5)

Who Said It?

Have you heard these biblical quotations? Do you know who said them? Look up the verses to find out.

"Am I my brother's keeper?"
A. Cain   B. Solomon   C. Abel
(See Genesis 4:9.)

"Prophets are not without honor, except in their hometown, and among their own kin, and in their own house."
A. Paul   B. Jesus   C. Matthew
(See Mark 6:4.)

"Beware of false prophets, who come to you in sheep's clothing but inwardly are ravenous wolves."
A. Moses   B. Peter   C. Jesus
(See Matthew 7:15.)

The Old Testament in the New Testament

Scholars have counted and recounted and come up with a different number each time when it comes to the number of Old Testament quotations found in the New Testament. One authority says he counted at least 224 quotations, while another says there are more than 295. Here are just a few from the New King James Version (NKJV) for you to compare:

Matthew 15:4a—"Honor your father and your mother." (Exodus 20:12; Deuteronomy 5:16)

Hebrews 8:8b-12—"Behold, the days are coming, says the Lord, when I will make a new covenant with the house of Israel and with the house of Judah—not according to the covenant that I made with their fathers in the day when I took them by the hand to lead them out of the land of Egypt; because they did not continue in My covenant, and I disregarded them, says the Lord. For this is the covenant that I will make with the house of Israel: After those days, says the Lord, I will put My laws in their mind and write them on their hearts; and I will be their God, and they shall by My people. None of them shall teach his neighbour, and none his brother, saying, Know the Lord, for all shall know Me, from the least to the greatest of them. For I will be merciful to their unrighteousness, and their sins and their lawless deeds I will remember no more." (Jeremiah 31:31-34)

Romans 9:12b—"The older shall serve the younger." (Genesis 25:23)

Romans 10:15b—"How beautiful are the feet of those who preach the gospel of peace, who bring glad tidings of good things!" (Isaiah 52:7; Nahum 1:15)

1 Corinthians 15:45b—"The first man Adam became a living being." (Genesis 2:7)

2 Corinthians 6:16b—"I will dwell in them and walk among them. I will be their God, and they shall be My people." (Leviticus 26:12; Jeremiah 32:38; Ezekiel 37:27)

Galatians 3:8b—"In you all the nations shall be blessed." (Genesis 12:3; 8:18; 22:18; 26:4; 28:14)

Galatians 3:11b—"The just shall live by faith." (Habakkuk 2:4)

Hebrews 4:4b—"And God rested on the seventh day from all His works." (Genesis 2:2)

Hebrews 13:6b—"The Lord is my helper; I will not fear. What can man do to me?" (Psalm 118:6)

Roll Call of Faith

The writer of Hebrews provides us with a list of names of faithful people of God. You can learn more about these persons by reading the passages given.

Abel: Hebrews 11:4—Because of his faith, he offered a more acceptable sacrifice than his brother, Cain, offered. (Genesis 4:3-10)

Enoch: Hebrews 11:5—He did not experience death because "he had pleased God." (Genesis 5:21-24)

Noah: Hebrews 11:7—He respected God's warning about the coming flood. (Genesis 6:13-22)

Abraham: Hebrews 11:8-12, 17-19—He obeyed God when God called him to set out for a place he did not know. He considered God to be faithful. He was ready to sacrifice his only son to God. (Genesis 12:1-8; 15:5-6: 17:19; 18:11-14; 21:2; 22:1-10, 17; 32:12)

Isaac: Hebrews 11:20—He invoked blessings upon the futures of his sons, Jacob and Esau. (Genesis 27:27-29, 39-40)

Jacob: Hebrews 11:21—He blessed each of the sons of Joseph, trusting the future even when he himself was dying. (Genesis 48:8-20)

Joseph: Hebrews 11:22—He looked ahead to the Exodus when he was dying. (Genesis 50:24-25; Exodus 13:19)

Moses: Hebrews 11:23-28—He chose to share the ill treatment suffered by the Hebrews rather than to enjoy the privileges of the Egyptians. He also held on to courage while leaving Egypt and observing the first Passover. (Exodus 2; 12:21-30)

Rahab: Hebrews 11:31—She was a prostitute of Jericho who survived its destruction because she hid two Israelite spies. (Joshua 2:1-21; 6:22-25)

Gideon, Barak, Samson, Jephthah, David, Samuel: Hebrews 11:32-34—They conquered kingdoms; administered justice; obtained the fulfillment of promises; escaped death by wild animals, fire, and sword; and achieved victories in battle although militarily weaker. (Judges 4–8; 11; 13–16; 1 Samuel 1–30; 2 Samuel; 1 Kings 1–2)

Jesus: Hebrews 12:2, 24—He endured the cross and is considered "the pioneer and perfecter of our faith," "the mediator of a new covenant."[1]

Biblical Origins

Many of the phrases that we hear in everyday language come from the Bible. What do the following phrases mean? Read the Bible verses to learn the origin of the phrases.

- doubting Thomas   *John 14:4; 20:24-29*
- forbidden fruit   *Genesis 3:3*
- raising Cain   *Genesis*
- wash your hands of the matter   *Matthew 27:24*
- practice what you preach   *Matthew 23:3*
- going the second mile   *Matthew 5:41*
- salt of the earth   *Matthew 5:13*
- a house divided   *Matthew 12:25; Luke 11:17*
- a man after his own heart   *1 Samuel 13:14*
- apple of my eye   *Deuteronomy 2:10; Zechariah 2:8*
- at my wit's end   *Psalm 107:27*

- blind leading the blind   *Matthew 15:14; Luke 6:39*
- by the skin of our teeth   *Job 19:20*
- can a leopard change his spots?   *Jeremiah 13:23*
- don't cast your pearls before swine   *Matthew 7:6*
- drop in the bucket   *Isaiah 40:15*
- eat, drink, and be merry   *Ecclesiastes 8:15*
- eye for an eye   *Exodus 21:24; Leviticus 24:20; Deuteronomy 19:21; Matthew 5:38*
- fight the good fight   *1 Timothy 6:12*
- he gave up the ghost   *Luke 23:46*
- many are called, but few are chosen   *Matthew 22:14*
- man shall not live by bread alone   *Deuteronomy 8:3; Matthew 4:4*
- more blessed to give than to receive   *Acts 20:35*
- out of the mouths of babes   *Psalm 8:2*
- pride goes before a fall   *Proverbs 16:19*
- put your house in order   *2 Kings 20:1; Isaiah 38:1*
- red sky at morning   *Matthew 16:3*
- signs of the times   *Matthew 16:3*
- the truth will make you free   *John 8:32*
- there's nothing new under the sun   *Ecclesiastes 1:9*
- thorn in the flesh   *2 Corinthians 12:7*
- to everything there is a season   *Ecclesiastes 3:1*
- twinkling of an eye   *1 Corinthians 15:52*
- where there is no vision, the people perish   *Proverbs 29:18*

What Is a Jacob's Ladder?

In Genesis 28:12-13, Jacob dreamed of a ladder that stretched to heaven. A ladder made of rope and wooden rungs and those made of metal chain, like the kinds used on ships, are called Jacob's ladders.

Every Jot and Tittle?

Has anyone ever asked you to pay attention to every "jot and tittle"? Did you know what they meant? How about where the term originated? Read Matthew 5:18.

The jot was the Hebrew character known as the *yodh*. Similar to the apostrophe, it was the smallest Hebrew letter. A tittle was a small mark placed on the edge of some letters to distinguish them from other letters.

So What's the Ark, and Where Is It?

The ark is not the boat that Noah built. It is the ark of the covenant. This was a large, beautiful box that Moses was given instructions to build by God. Its purpose was to house the Ten Commandments, the staff of Aaron (Moses' brother), and manna. The ark's whereabouts can be traced in Scripture from the time that it was built under the guidance of Moses through the time that the Babylonians destroyed Jerusalem. At that point, it disappeared and was presumed destroyed by the Babylonians.

The Bible and Literature

Poets including Chaucer, Lord Byron, William Wordsworth, Tennyson, Longfellow, and many others have found great inspiration in the Bible. Here are just three examples:

"A Prayer in Spring" by **Robert Frost**[2]
> For this is love and nothing else is love,
> The which it is reserved for God above

"Evangeline" by **Henry Wadsworth Longfellow**[3]
> Lo! where the crucified Christ from his cross is gazing upon you!
> See! in those sorrowful eyes what meekness and holy compassion!

"To a Waterfowl" by **William Cullen Bryant**[4]
There is a Power whose care
Teaches thy way along that pathless coast—

On the other hand, contemporary novelists have based entire novels on biblical themes. Just for example:

The Grapes of Wrath by John Steinbeck
The Song of Solomon by Toni Morrison
Moby Dick by Herman Melville
Lord of the Flies by William Golding
The Scarlet Letter by Nathaniel Hawthorne
Uncle Tom's Cabin by Harriet Beecher Stowe

▶ *FAST FACT:* Literary scholars estimate that *Uncle Tom's Cabin* by Harriet Beecher Stowe contains roughly 100 quotations and references from the King James Version of the Bible.[5]

Shakespeare and the Bible

Undoubtedly, like other affluent children growing up in the sixteenth century, one of William Shakespeare's textbooks was the Holy Bible. Not only does he quote from the Bible in his poems and plays, he builds many plots and characters based on biblical teachings.[6]

Here are two examples:

"Be thou cursed Cain,
To slay thy brother Abel, if thou wilt."
From *I Henry VI*. 1, 3[7]

"Blessed are the peacemakers on earth."
From *2 Henry IV*.[8]

In his plays alone, Shakespeare included the name of God more than 700 times.

For example:

"God above deal between me and thee."
From *Macbeth* 4, 3[9]

"And God shall be my hope, my stay, my guide and lantern to my feet."
From *2 Henry VI*. 2, 3[10]

▶ *FAST FACT:* According to literary scholars, Shakespeare quoted from Matthew 151 times and from the Psalms 137 times.[11]

Hymns

Singing hymns isn't a new thing. Take a look at these verses to see a few of the many occasions when people sang hymns:

Matthew 26:30—"When they had sung the hymn, they went out to the Mount of Olives."
Acts 16:25—"About midnight Paul and Silas were praying and singing hymns to God, and the other prisoners were listening to them."
Ephesians 5:19—"Sing psalms and hymns and spiritual songs among yourselves, singing and making melody to the Lord in your hearts."

Colossians 3:16—"With gratitude in your hearts sing psalms, hymns, and spiritual songs to God."

Psalm 95:2—"Let us come into his presence with thanksgiving; let us make a joyful noise to him with songs of praise!"

Jeremiah 20:13—"Sing to the Lord; praise the Lord! / For he has delivered the life of the needy from the hands of evildoers."

The Bible and Art

For centuries, Bible stories have been a popular subject of artist interpretation. From Michaelangelo's paintings on the ceiling of the Sistine Chapel to Raphael's famous Madonnas, and beyond, museum and gallery goers can appreciate many Bible stories through art. Here are a few items you might find along the way.

Leonardo da Vinci[12]
"John the Baptist"
oil on panel, ca. 1513/16
Musée du Louvre, Paris

"The Adoration of the Magi"
oil on panel, 1481–82
Galleria degli Uffizi, Florence

"The Last Supper (1)"
oil and tempera on plaster, ca. 1495/98
Santa Maria delle Grazie, Milan

·"The Last Supper (2)"
oil and tempera on plaster, ca. 1495/98
Santa Maria delle Grazie, Milan

Michelangelo[13]
Scenes from Genesis (the ceiling)
fresco, 1508–1512
Sistine Chapel, Vatican City

Raphael[14]
"The Healing of the Lame Man"
tempera on paper on linen, c. 1516
Victoria and Albert Museum, London

"The Miraculous Draught of Fishes"
tapestry, ca. 1519
Vatican Museums, Vatican City

"The Prophet Isaiah"
fresco, 1511–1512
Sant'Agostino, Rome

Rembrandt[15]
"Boaz Pouring Six Measures of Barley Into Ruth's Veil"
pen drawing, c. 1650
Rijksprentenkabinet, Amsterdam

"Daniel in the Lions' Den"
drawing with pen and brush, ca. 1652
Rijksprentenkabinet, Amsterdam

"Doubting Thomas"
oil on panel, 1634
Pushkin Museum, Moscow

"The Risen Christ Appearing to Mary Magdalen"
oil on canvas, 1638
Royal Collection, Buckingham Palace, London

▶ *FAST FACT:* Rembrandt created some 300 biblical drawings, paintings, and sculptures.[16]

Vincent Van Gogh
"The Raising of Lazarus"
oil on canvas, 1890
Van Gogh Museum, Amsterdam

▶ *FAST FACT:* The statue of David by Michelangelo is probably the most famous statue in the world. Another of Michelangelo's popular sculptures is a statue of Moses that was made for the Tomb of Julius II.[17]

Michelangelo[18]
"David"
marble, 1501–1504
Galleria dell'Accademia, Florence

"Pietà"
marble, 1499
Vatican Museums, Vatican City

▶ *FAST FACT:* The statue of David by Donatello was the first free-standing nude statue in the Christian era.[19]

Movies

A number of scriptwriters and movie producers have focused on biblical stories. Some of the movies have brought about great controversy and many have won critical and popular acclaim. Here are a few classic movies with a biblical focus:

The Ten Commandments (1956; starring Charlton Heston, Yul Brynner)
Friendly Persuasion (1956; starring Gary Cooper)
King David (1985; PG-13; starring Richard Gere)
Prince of Egypt (1998; PG; starring Val Kilmer)
The Apostle (1998; PG; starring Robert Duvall)
Joshua (2002; G; starring Tony Goldwyn, F. Murray Abraham)
The Passion of Christ (2004; R; starring James Caviezel)
One Night with the King (2006; PG; starring Peter O'Toole, Tiffany Dupont, Omar Sharif)
The Nativity Story (2006; PG; starring Keisha Castle-Hughes, Oscar Isaac)

---

[1]Adapted from *Get Acquainted With Your Bible.* Copyright © 1993 Abingdon Press. Used by permission.

[2]*The Poetry of Robert Frost: The Collected Poems, Complete and Unabridged,* Edward Connery Lathern, ed. (Henry Holt, 1969); p. 12.

[3]*Henry Wadsworth Longfellow: Poems and Other Writings,* J.D. McClatchy, ed. (Library of America, 2000); p. 81.

[4]*William Cullen Bryant: An American Voice*, Frank Gado, ed. (Antoca Press, 2006); p. 39.

[5]"The Bible and Uncle Tom's Cabin" (Stephen Railton and the University of Virginia, 2007); www.iath.virginia.edu/utc/christn/kjb_utc.html.

[6]Christian History Institute; http://chi.gospelcom.net/DAILYF/2003/04/daily-04-23-2003.shtml

[7]*The Bible in Shakespeare*, by Prof. Carl Ackermann (Folcroft Library Editions, 1971); p. 61.

[8]Ackermann; p. 61.

[9]Ackermann; p.120.

[10]Ackermann; p. 120.

[11]Christian History Institute; see note 5.

[12]"Biblical Art by Leonardo da Vinci" (Art and the Bible, 2005-08); http://www.artbible.info/art/work/leonardo-da-vinci.html

[13]"Biblical Art by Michelangelo Buonarroti" (Art and the Bible, 2005-08); http://www.artbible.info/art/work/michelangelo-buonarroti.html.

[14]"Biblical Art by Raphael" (Art and the Bible, 2005-08); http://www.artbible.info/art/work/raphael.html.

[15]"Biblical Art by Rembrandt Harmensz. van Rijn" (Art and the Bible, 2005-08); http://www.artbible.info/art/work/rembrandt-harmensz-van-rijn.html.

[16]"Rembrandt's Biblical Work" (Art and the Bible, 2005-08); http://www.artbible.info/art/rembrandt-biblical-work.html.

[17]"Statue of David by Michelangelo"; http://www.statue.com/statue-of-david.html.

[18]"Biblical Art by Michelangelo Buonarroti"; see note 12.

[19]"Statue of David by Michelangelo"; see note 16.

Read the Bible
in a Year

Here is a suggested plan to read the entire Bible through in a year.[1] It is very simple to follow—you may begin on January 1 or simply Day 1 if you are starting on a different date. It can take as little as 5-10 minutes per day. Of course, you may want to spend longer and include time for reflection and journaling as the Scriptures speak to you.

After over twenty centuries, the Word of God is still alive and powerful and speaks to us. In this Word are glimpses of God's truth and redeeming grace, God's plan for the world and how you can find your place in it. Enjoy your year with the Word of God.

Day 1	Jan. 1	Gen. 1; Ps. 1, 2	Day 18	Jan. 18	Gen. 37, 38; Ps. 21
Day 2	Jan. 2	Gen. 2; Ps. 3, 4	Day 19	Jan. 19	Gen. 39, 40; Ps. 22
Day 3	Jan. 3	Gen. 3, 4; Ps. 5, 6	Day 20	Jan. 20	Gen. 41, 42; Ps. 23, 24
Day 4	Jan. 4	Gen. 5, 6; Ps. 7	Day 21	Jan. 21	Gen. 43, 44, 45
Day 5	Jan. 5	Gen. 7, 8; Ps. 8	Day 22	Jan. 22	Gen. 46, 47, 48
Day 6	Jan. 6	Gen. 9, 10, 11; Ps. 9	Day 23	Jan. 23	Gen. 49, 50; Ps. 25
Day 7	Jan. 7	Gen. 12, 13; Ps. 10	Day 24	Jan. 24	Ex. 1, 2; Ps. 26, 27
Day 8	Jan. 8	Gen. 14, 15; Ps. 11	Day 25	Jan. 25	Ex. 3, 4; Ps. 28
Day 9	Jan. 9	Gen. 16, 17; Ps. 12	Day 26	Jan. 26	Ex. 5, 6, 7
Day 10	Jan. 10	Gen. 18, 19; Ps. 13, 14	Day 27	Jan. 27	Ex. 8, 9, 10; Ps. 29
Day 11	Jan. 11	Gen. 20, 21; Ps. 15	Day 28	Jan. 28	Ex. 11, 12; Ps. 30
Day 12	Jan. 12	Gen. 22, 23; Ps. 16	Day 29	Jan. 29	Ex. 13, 14, 15
Day 13	Jan. 13	Gen. 24, 25; Ps. 17, 18	Day 30	Jan. 30	Ex. 16, 17, 18
Day 14	Jan. 14	Gen. 26, 27; Ps. 19	Day 31	Jan. 31	Ex. 19, 20; Ps. 31, 32
Day 15	Jan. 15	Gen. 28, 29, 30	Day 32	Feb. 1	Ex. 21, 22, 23
Day 16	Jan. 16	Gen. 31, 32, 33	Day 33	Feb. 2	Ex. 24, 25, 26
Day 17	Jan. 17	Gen. 34, 35, 36; Ps. 20	Day 34	Feb. 3	Ex. 27, 28, 29, 30

Day 35	Feb. 4	Ex. 31, 32, 33		Day 82	Mar. 23	Judg. 1, 2, 3
Day 36	Feb. 5	Ex. 34, 35, 36		Day 83	Mar. 24	Judg. 4, 5; Ps. 56, 57
Day 37	Feb. 6	Ex. 37, 38, 39, 40		Day 84	Mar. 25	Judg. 6, 7, 8
Day 38	Feb. 7	Lev. 1, 2, 3		Day 85	Mar. 26	Judg. 9, 10, 11
Day 39	Feb. 8	Lev. 4, 5, 6		Day 86	Mar. 27	Judg. 12, 13, 14
Day 40	Feb. 9	Lev. 7, 8, 9		Day 87	Mar. 28	Judg. 15, 16; Ps. 58, 59
Day 41	Feb. 10	Lev. 10, 11; Ps. 33, 34		Day 88	Mar. 29	Judg. 17, 18, 19
Day 42	Feb. 11	Lev. 12, 13; Ps. 35		Day 89	Mar. 30	Judg. 20, 21; Ps. 60
Day 43	Feb. 12	Lev. 14, 15; Ps. 36		Day 90	Mar. 31	Ruth 1, 2, 3, 4
Day 44	Feb. 13	Lev. 16, 17, 18		Day 91	Apr. 1	1 Sam. 1, 2, 3
Day 45	Feb. 14	Lev. 19, 20, 21; Ps. 37		Day 92	Apr. 2	1 Sam. 4, 5, 6
Day 46	Feb. 15	Lev. 22, 23, 24		Day 93	Apr. 3	1 Sam. 7, 8, 9
Day 47	Feb. 16	Lev. 25, 26, 27		Day 94	Apr. 4	1 Sam. 10, 11, 12; Ps. 61
Day 48	Feb. 17	Num. 1, 2, 3; Ps. 38		Day 95	Apr. 5	1 Sam. 13, 14, 15
Day 49	Feb. 18	Num. 4, 5, 6		Day 96	Apr. 6	1 Sam. 16, 17, 18
Day 50	Feb. 19	Num. 7, 8; Ps. 39		Day 97	Apr. 7	1 Sam. 19, 20, 21, 22
Day 51	Feb. 20	Num. 9, 10; Ps. 40		Day 98	Apr. 8	1 Sam. 23, 24, 25
Day 52	Feb. 21	Num. 11, 12; Ps. 41, 42		Day 99	Apr. 9	1 Sam. 26, 27, 28
Day 53	Feb. 22	Num. 13, 14, 15		Day 100	Apr. 10	1 Sam. 29, 30, 31
Day 54	Feb. 23	Num. 16, 17, 18		Day 101	Apr. 11	2 Sam. 1, 2, 3; Ps. 62
Day 55	Feb. 24	Num. 19, 20; Ps. 43, 44		Day 102	Apr. 12	2 Sam. 4, 5, 6
Day 56	Feb. 25	Num. 21; Ps. 45, 46		Day 103	Apr. 13	2 Sam. 7, 8, 9
Day 57	Feb. 26	Num. 22, 23, 24		Day 104	Apr. 14	2 Sam. 10, 11, 12; Ps. 63
Day 58	Feb. 27	Num. 25, 26, 27		Day 105	Apr. 15	2 Sam. 13, 14, 15
Day 59	Feb. 28	Num. 28, 29, 30, 31		Day 106	Apr. 16	2 Sam. 16, 17, 18
Day 60	Mar. 1	Num. 32, 33, 34		Day 107	Apr. 17	2 Sam. 19, 20, 21
Day 61	Mar. 2	Num. 35, 36; Ps. 47		Day 108	Apr. 18	2 Sam. 22, 23, 24; Ps. 64
Day 62	Mar. 3	Deut. 1, 2, 3: Ps. 48		Day 109	Apr. 19	1 Kings 1, 2, 3
Day 63	Mar. 4	Deut. 4, 5: Ps. 49		Day 110	Apr. 20	1 Kings 4, 5, 6
Day 64	Mar. 5	Deut. 6, 7, 8		Day 111	Apr. 21	1 Kings 7, 8, 9; Ps. 65
Day 65	Mar. 6	Deut. 9, 10, 11		Day 112	Apr. 22	1 Kings 10, 11; Ps. 66
Day 66	Mar. 7	Deut. 12, 13, 14: Ps. 50		Day 113	Apr. 23	1 Kings 12, 13, 14
Day 67	Mar. 8	Deut. 15, 16, 17		Day 114	Apr. 24	1 Kings 15, 16; Ps. 67
Day 68	Mar. 9	Deut. 18, 19, 20		Day 115	Apr. 25	1 Kings 17, 18; Ps. 68, 69
Day 69	Mar. 10	Deut. 21, 22, 23: Ps. 51		Day 116	Apr. 26	1 Kings 19, 20; Ps. 70
Day 70	Mar. 11	Deut. 24, 25, 26		Day 117	Apr. 27	1 Kings 21, 226; Ps. 71
Day 71	Mar. 12	Deut. 27, 28, 29		Day 118	Apr. 28	2 Kings 1, 2, 3; Ps. 72
Day 72	Mar. 13	Deut. 30, 31, 32		Day 119	Apr. 29	2 Kings 4, 5; Ps. 73
Day 73	Mar. 14	Deut. 33, 34; Ps. 52, 53		Day 120	Apr. 30	2 Kings 6, 7, 8
Day 74	Mar. 15	Josh. 1, 2, 3		Day 121	May 1	2 Kings 9, 10, 11
Day 75	Mar. 16	Josh. 4, 5, 6		Day 122	May 2	2 Kings 12, 13, 14; Ps. 74
Day 76	Mar. 17	Josh. 7, 8, 9; Ps. 54		Day 123	May 3	2 Kings 15, 16, 17
Day 77	Mar. 18	Josh. 10, 11, 12		Day 124	May 4	2 Kings 18, 19, 20
Day 78	Mar. 19	Josh. 13, 14, 15		Day 125	May 5	2 Kings 21, 22, 23; Ps. 75
Day 79	Mar. 20	Josh. 16, 17, 18		Day 126	May 6	2 Kings 24, 25; Ps. 76
Day 80	Mar. 21	Josh. 19, 20, 21; Ps. 55		Day 127	May 7	1 Chr. 1, 2, 3
Day 81	Mar. 22	Josh. 22, 23, 24		Day 128	May 8	1 Chr. 4, 5; Ps. 77

106

Day 129	May 9	1 Chr. 6, 7; Ps. 78, 79
Day 130	May 10	1 Chr. 8, 9; Ps. 80
Day 131	May 11	1 Chr. 10, 11, 12
Day 132	May 12	1 Chr. 13, 14, 15; Ps. 81
Day 133	May 13	1 Chr. 16, 17, 18
Day 134	May 14	1 Chr. 19, 20, 21
Day 135	May 15	1 Chr. 22, 23, 24
Day 136	May 16	1 Chr. 25, 26, 27; Ps. 82
Day 137	May 17	1 Chr. 28, 29; Ps. 83
Day 138	May 18	2 Chr. 1, 2, 3
Day 139	May 19	2 Chr. 4, 5, 6, 7
Day 140	May 20	2 Chr. 8, 9; Ps. 84
Day 141	May 21	2 Chr. 10, 11, 12
Day 142	May 22	2 Chr. 13, 14, 15
Day 143	May 23	2 Chr. 16, 17, 18; Ps. 85
Day 144	May 24	2 Chr. 19, 20, 21
Day 145	May 25	2 Chr. 22, 23, 24
Day 146	May 26	2 Chr. 25, 26; Ps. 86, 87
Day 147	May 27	2 Chr. 27, 28; Ps. 88
Day 148	May 28	2 Chr. 29, 30, 31, 32
Day 149	May 29	2 Chr. 33, 34; Ps. 89
Day 150	May 30	2 Chr. 35, 36; Ps. 90
Day 151	May 31	Ezra 1, 2, 3
Day 152	Jun. 1	Ezra 4, 5, 6
Day 153	Jun. 2	Ezra 7, 8; Ps. 91, 92
Day 154	Jun. 3	Ezra 9, 10; Ps. 93
Day 155	Jun. 4	Neh. 1, 2, 3
Day 156	Jun. 5	Neh. 4, 5, 6
Day 157	Jun. 6	Neh. 7, 8; Ps. 94, 95
Day 158	Jun. 7	Neh. 9, 10; Ps. 96
Day 159	Jun. 8	Neh. 11, 12, 13
Day 160	Jun. 9	Esth. 1, 2, 3: Ps. 97
Day 161	Jun. 10	Esth. 4, 5, 6
Day 162	Jun. 11	Esth. 7, 8, 9, 10
Day 163	Jun. 12	Job 1, 2, 3
Day 164	Jun. 13	Job 4, 5, 6
Day 165	Jun. 14	Job 7, 8, 9
Day 166	Jun. 15	Job 10, 11, 12
Day 167	Jun. 16	Job 13, 14, 15; Ps. 98
Day 168	Jun. 17	Job 16, 17, 18
Day 169	Jun. 18	Job 19, 20, 21
Day 170	Jun. 19	Job 22, 23, 24
Day 171	Jun. 20	Job 25, 26, 27, 28
Day 172	Jun. 21	Job 29, 30, 31
Day 173	Jun. 22	Job 32, 33, 34
Day 174	Jun. 23	Job 35, 36, 37; Ps. 99
Day 175	Jun. 24	Job 38, 39, 40, 41
Day 176	Jun. 25	Job 42; Ps. 100, 101
Day 177	Jun. 26	Eccl. 1, 2, 3
Day 178	Jun. 27	Eccl. 4, 5, 6
Day 179	Jun. 28	Eccl. 7, 8, 9
Day 180	Jun. 29	Eccl. 10, 11, 12
Day 181	Jun. 30	S. of Sol. 1, 2, 3; Ps. 102
Day 182	Jul. 1	S. of Sol. 4, 5, 6
Day 183	Jul. 2	S. of Sol. 7, 8; Ps. 103
Day 184	Jul. 3	Isa. 1, 2, 3
Day 185	Jul. 4	Isa. 4, 5, 6; Ps. 104
Day 186	Jul. 5	Isa. 7, 8, 9
Day 187	Jul. 6	Isa. 10, 11, 12
Day 188	Jul. 7	Isa. 13, 14, 15, 16
Day 189	Jul. 8	Isa. 17, 18, 19
Day 190	Jul. 9	Isa. 20, 21, 22, 23
Day 191	Jul. 10	Isa. 24, 25, 26
Day 192	Jul. 11	Isa. 27, 28, 29
Day 193	Jul. 12	Isa. 30, 31, 32
Day 194	Jul. 13	Isa. 33, 34, 35
Day 195	Jul. 14	Isa. 36, 37; Ps. 105, 106
Day 196	Jul. 15	Isa. 38, 39; Ps. 107
Day 197	Jul. 16	Isa. 40, 41, 42
Day 198	Jul. 17	Isa. 43, 44, 45
Day 199	Jul. 18	Isa. 46, 47, 48, 49
Day 200	Jul. 19	Isa. 50, 51; Ps. 108
Day 201	Jul. 20	Isa. 52, 53, 54
Day 202	Jul. 21	Isa. 55, 56, 57; Ps. 109
Day 203	Jul. 22	Isa. 58, 59, 60
Day 204	Jul. 23	Isa. 61, 62, 63
Day 205	Jul. 24	Isa. 64, 65, 66
Day 206	Jul. 25	Jer. 1, 2, 3; Ps. 110
Day 207	Jul. 26	Jer. 4, 5, 6
Day 208	Jul. 27	Jer. 7, 8, 9
Day 209	Jul. 28	Jer. 10, 11, 12; Ps. 111
Day 210	Jul. 29	Jer. 13, 14, 15
Day 211	Jul. 30	Jer. 16, 17, 18
Day 212	Jul. 31	Jer. 19, 20, 21
Day 213	Aug. 1	Jer. 22, 23, 24; Ps. 112
Day 214	Aug. 2	Jer. 25, 26, 27
Day 215	Aug. 3	Jer. 28, 29, 30
Day 216	Aug. 4	Jer. 31, 32, 33; Ps. 113
Day 217	Aug. 5	Jer. 34, 35, 36
Day 218	Aug. 6	Jer. 37, 38, 39
Day 219	Aug. 7	Jer. 40, 41, 42, 43
Day 220	Aug. 8	Jer. 44, 45; Ps. 114
Day 221	Aug. 9	Jer. 46, 47, 48, 49
Day 222	Aug. 10	Jer. 50, 51, 52

Day 223	Aug. 11	Lam. 1, 2; Ps. 115
Day 224	Aug. 12	Lam. 3, 4, 5
Day 225	Aug. 13	Ezek. 1, 2, 3
Day 226	Aug. 14	Ezek. 4, 5, 6
Day 227	Aug. 15	Ezek. 7, 8, 9, 10
Day 228	Aug. 16	Ezek. 11, 12, 13
Day 229	Aug. 17	Ezek. 14, 15, 16
Day 230	Aug. 18	Ezek. 17, 18, 19; Ps. 116
Day 231	Aug. 19	Ezek. 20, 21, 22
Day 232	Aug. 20	Ezek. 23, 24, 25
Day 233	Aug. 21	Ezek. 26, 27, 28
Day 234	Aug. 22	Ezek. 29, 30, 31, 32
Day 235	Aug. 23	Ezek. 33, 34; Psalm 117
Day 236	Aug. 24	Ezek. 35, 36, 37
Day 237	Aug. 25	Ezek. 38, 39; Ps. 118, 119:1-24
Day 238	Aug. 26	Ezek. 40, 41, 42
Day 239	Aug. 27	Ezek. 43, 44, 45
Day 240	Aug. 28	Ezek. 46, 47, 48
Day 241	Aug. 29	Dan. 1, 2, 3; Ps. 119:25-48
Day 242	Aug. 30	Dan. 4, 5, 6
Day 243	Aug. 31	Dan. 7, 8, 9
Day 244	Sept. 1	Dan. 10, 11, 12; Ps. 119:49-72
Day 245	Sept. 2	Hos. 1, 2, 3
Day 246	Sept. 3	Hos. 4, 5, 6
Day 247	Sept. 4	Hos. 7, 8, 9
Day 248	Sept. 5	Hos. 10, 11, 12
Day 249	Sept. 6	Hos. 13, 14; Ps. 119:73-120
Day 250	Sept. 7	Joel 1, 2, 3
Day 251	Sept. 8	Amos 1, 2, 3; Ps. 119:121-144
Day 252	Sept. 9	Amos 4, 5, 6
Day 253	Sept. 10	Amos 7, 8, 9; Obad.
Day 254	Sept. 11	Jon. 1, 2, 3, 4
Day 255	Sept. 12	Mic. 1, 2, 3
Day 256	Sept. 13	Mic. 4, 5, 6
Day 257	Sept. 14	Mic. 7; Ps. 119:145-176, 120
Day 258	Sept. 15	Nah. 1, 2, 3; Ps. 121
Day 259	Sept. 16	Hab. 1, 2, 3
Day 260	Sept. 17	Zeph. 1, 2, 3
Day 261	Sept. 18	Hag. 1, 2; Ps. 122
Day 262	Sept. 19	Zech. 1, 2, 3; Ps. 123
Day 263	Sept. 20	Zech. 4, 5, 6
Day 264	Sept. 21	Zech. 7, 8, 9, 10
Day 265	Sept. 22	Zech. 11, 12, 13, 14
Day 266	Sept. 23	Mal. 1, 2, 3, 4
Day 267	Sept. 24	Matt. 1, 2; Ps. 124
Day 268	Sept. 25	Matt. 3, 4; Ps. 125
Day 269	Sept. 26	Matt. 5, 6, 7
Day 270	Sept. 27	Matt. 8, 9; Ps. 126
Day 271	Sept. 28	Matt. 10, 11, 12
Day 272	Sept. 29	Matt. 13, 14; Ps. 127
Day 273	Sept. 30	Matt. 15, 16, 17
Day 274	Oct. 1	Matt. 18, 19, 20
Day 275	Oct. 2	Matt. 21, 22, 23
Day 276	Oct. 3	Matt. 24, 25; Ps. 128, 129
Day 277	Oct. 4	Matt. 26, 27, 28
Day 278	Oct. 5	Mark 1, 2, 3
Day 279	Oct. 6	Mark 4, 5, 6
Day 280	Oct. 7	Mark 7, 8, 9
Day 281	Oct. 8	Mark 10, 11, 12
Day 282	Oct. 9	Mark 13, 14; Ps. 130, 131
Day 283	Oct. 10	Mark 15, 16; Ps. 132, 133
Day 284	Oct. 11	Luke 1, 2, 3
Day 285	Oct. 12	Luke 4, 5, 6
Day 286	Oct. 13	Luke 7, 8; Ps. 134, 135
Day 287	Oct. 14	Luke 9, 10, 11
Day 288	Oct. 15	Luke 12, 13, 14
Day 289	Oct. 16	Luke 15, 16; Ps. 136
Day 290	Oct. 17	Luke 17, 18, 19; Ps. 137
Day 291	Oct. 18	Luke 20, 21; Ps. 138
Day 292	Oct. 19	Luke 22, 23, 24
Day 293	Oct. 20	John 1, 2, 3; Ps. 139
Day 294	Oct. 21	John 4, 5; Ps. 140
Day 295	Oct. 22	John 6, 7; Ps. 141
Day 296	Oct. 23	John 8, 9; Ps. 142
Day 297	Oct. 24	John 10, 11; Ps. 143
Day 298	Oct. 25	John 12, 13; Ps. 144
Day 299	Oct. 26	John 14, 15, 16, 17
Day 300	Oct. 27	John 18, 19; Ps. 145, 146
Day 301	Oct. 28	John 20, 21; Ps. 147
Day 302	Oct. 29	Acts 1, 2, 3
Day 303	Oct. 30	Acts 4, 5; Ps. 148
Day 304	Oct. 31	Acts 6, 7; Ps. 149
Day 305	Nov. 1	Acts 8, 9, 10
Day 306	Nov. 2	Acts 11, 12; Ps. 150
Day 307	Nov. 3	Acts 13, 14, 15; Prov. 1
Day 308	Nov. 4	Acts 16, 17, 18
Day 309	Nov. 5	Acts 19, 20, 21
Day 310	Nov. 6	Acts 22, 23, 24
Day 311	Nov. 7	Acts 25, 26; Prov. 2

Day 312	Nov. 8	Acts 27, 28; Prov. 3		Day 339	Dec. 5	1 Tim. 1, 2, 3
Day 313	Nov. 9	Rom. 1, 2, 3		Day 340	Dec. 6	1 Tim. 4, 5, 6
Day 314	Nov. 10	Rom. 4, 5, 6		Day 341	Dec. 7	2 Tim. 1, 2, 3, 4
Day 315	Nov. 11	Rom. 7, 8; Prov. 4		Day 342	Dec. 8	Tit. 1, 2, 3; Prov. 15
Day 316	Nov. 12	Rom. 9, 10, 11		Day 343	Dec. 9	Philem.; Prov. 16, 17
Day 317	Nov. 13	Rom. 12, 13, 14		Day 344	Dec. 10	Heb. 1, 2, 3
Day 318	Nov. 14	Rom. 15, 16; Prov. 5		Day 345	Dec. 11	Heb. 4, 5, 6
Day 319	Nov. 15	1 Cor. 1, 2, 3		Day 346	Dec. 12	Heb. 7, 8, 9
Day 320	Nov. 16	1 Cor. 4, 5, 6, 7		Day 347	Dec. 13	Heb. 10, 11; Prov. 18
Day 321	Nov. 17	1 Cor. 8, 9, 10		Day 348	Dec. 14	Heb. 12, 13; Prov. 19, 20
Day 322	Nov. 18	1 Cor. 11, 12, 13, 14		Day 349	Dec. 15	Jam. 1, 2, 3
Day 323	Nov. 18	1 Cor. 15, 16; Prov. 6		Day 350	Dec. 16	Jam. 4, 5; Prov. 21
Day 324	Nov. 20	2 Cor. 1, 2, 3		Day 351	Dec. 17	1 Pet. 1, 2, Prov. 22
Day 325	Nov. 21	2 Cor. 4, 5, 6; Prov. 7		Day 352	Dec. 18	1 Pet. 3, 4, 5
Day 326	Nov. 22	2 Cor. 7, 8, 9		Day 353	Dec. 19	2 Pet. 1, 2, 3; Prov. 23
Day 327	Nov. 23	2 Cor. 10, 11; Prov. 8		Day 354	Dec. 20	1 John 1, 2; Prov. 24
Day 328	Nov. 24	2 Cor. 12, 13; Prov. 9		Day 355	Dec. 21	I John 3, 4, 5; Prov. 25
Day 329	Nov. 25	Galatians 1, 2; Prov. 10		Day 356	Dec. 22	2 John; 3 John; Prov. 26
Day 330	Nov. 26	Galatians 3, 4, 5, 6		Day 357	Dec. 23	Jude; Prov. 27, 28
Day 331	Nov. 27	Ephesians 1, 2, 3		Day 358	Dec. 24	Rev. 1, 2, 3
Day 332	Nov. 28	Ephesians 4, 5, 6		Day 359	Dec. 25	Rev. 4, 5; Prov. 29
Day 333	Nov. 29	Philippians 1, 2; Prov. 11		Day 360	Dec. 26	Rev. 6, 7; Prov. 30
Day 334	Nov. 30	Philippians 3, 4; Prov. 12		Day 361	Dec. 27	Rev. 8, 9, 10
Day 335	Dec. 1	Col. 1, 2; Prov. 13		Day 362	Dec. 28	Rev. 11, 12, 13
Day 336	Dec. 2	Col. 3, 4; Prov. 14		Day 363	Dec. 29	Rev. 14, 15, 16, 17
Day 337	Dec. 3	1 Thess. 1, 2, 3, 4, 5		Day 364	Dec. 30	Rev. 18, 19, 20; Prov. 31
Day 338	Dec. 4	2 Thess. 1, 2, 3		Day 365	Dec. 31	Rev. 21, 22

[1]Suggested reading selections taken from *The Grand Sweep: 365 Days From Genesis Through Revelation*, by J. Ellsworth Kalas (Abingdon Press, 1996).